THE EVERYTHING® DREAMS BOOK

THE
EVERYTHING®
DREAMS BOOK

From fantasies to nightmares, what your
dreams mean, how to remember them,
and how they affect your everyday life

Trish and Rob MacGregor

Adams Media Corporation
Avon, Massachusetts

An Everything® Series Book.
Everything® and everything.com® are registered trademarks of Adams Media Corporation.

Published by Adams Media Corporation
57 Littlefield Street, Avon, MA 02322. U.S.A.
www.adamsmedia.com

ISBN: 1-55850-806-6

Printed in the United States of America.

J I H G

Library of Congress Cataloging-in-Publication Data
McGregor, T.J.
The everything dreams book / Trish and Rob MacGregor. — 1st ed.
p.   cm. — (The everything series)
ISBN 1–55850–806–6 (pbk. : alk. paper)
1. Dream interpretation. 2. Dreams. I. MacGregor, Rob. II. Title. III. Series.
BF1091.M315   1997
15.6'3—dc21   97–24590
                                                                        CIP

Illustrations by Barry Littmann

This book is available at quantity discounts for bulk purchases.
For information, call 1-800-872-5627.

Visit the entire Everything® series at everything.com

With love to Megan,
who found the unicorn in her dreams

CONTENTS

PART TWO

DREAM TECHNIQUES

PART THREE

THE FAR SIDE OF DREAMING

PART FOUR
A DREAM GLOSSARY

INTRODUCTION

Why Pay Attention to Dreams?

Dreams are a reservoir of knowledge and experience, yet they are often overlooked as a vehicle for exploring reality.

—Tibetan teacher Tarthang Tulku, *Openness Mind*

★　　★　　★

It's a spooky house, almost Gothic in appearance, with several floors, turrets, and large, oddly-shaped windows. It reminds me of something from a Stephen King novel, that kind of eerie.

The first time I see it, it's night, and I'm standing in front of the house, looking up at it, and I don't want to go inside. It scares me. There seems to be something forbidding about it. It stands alone, quite isolated, in a clearing that's embraced by trees. I can't see the trees in any detail because it's too dark, but my impression is that they're huge, ancient, like sentient beings. They cast tremendous shadows.

I don't remember entering the house, but suddenly I'm walking around inside, on the first floor. I like the soft lighting, the tall ceilings, the quiet grace, the wide, winding staircase to the second floor. And there's so much space. I don't feel the least bit threatened or spooked at this point; I'm enthralled, curious, eager to explore.

I climb the stairs to the second floor and realize the house is structured much differently than I thought. Instead of just two stories, there appear to be several split levels that don't show from the outside.

One of these split levels consists of a single room with throw rugs on the wooden floor, a wall of glass that looks out into the trees, and furniture that is simple but unusual. There's a chair, for instance, that is suspended from the ceiling by ropes, and a white stone coffee table with engravings on it that look like petroglyphs. Shelves of books line one of the walls from floor to ceiling.

Another elevated room connects to a long corridor that intrigues me. As I walk into it, the corridor turns into a tunnel and slopes steeply downward. At one point, it becomes as smooth as a slide and I slide down it, into what I know is a basement.

This is where the dream becomes something else, something darker. I'm facing a heavy metal door. It isn't locked, not in any way I can perceive. I can see the rust on it, feel its age, its weight, and I'm terrified of what's behind it. At this point, I wake up and realize I've had this dream before.

★　　★　　★

Almost everyone has awakened from a startling dream and wondered for a few moments what it meant, and then forgotten about it as the day's activities began. But the residue of the dream clings to you. Was there a message in it for you?

Now imagine another scenario. You wake in the morning from the same dream, but this time you remember it in its entirety. You jot it down, then interpret it, and realize it addresses some of the major concerns in your life.

Janet L., the woman who related this dream, was in a transitional period in her life. Her career was undergoing an upheaval, her parents' health was declining, and she felt torn between the demands of her work and the needs of her family. In short, she stood at a crossroad.

Her interpretation of the dream was that the house symbolized the totality of who she was, what Swiss psychologist Carl Jung called the Self. The many rooms were the various facets of this Self—wife, mother, daughter, professional businesswoman, child, adult—all of the various roles she had played or was playing.

The ground floor was the Self she presented to the world, the way other people saw her—expansive, quiet, gracious, warm. The wide staircase, Janet felt, represented her conscious mind and the accessible way she offered this part of herself to other people.

The split levels of different rooms represented the different faces she wore. The furniture—simple but unusual—represented, she said, her family. She had dreamed of petroglyphs before, but not in this fashion; she

wasn't sure what they meant. The slide to the basement depicted the ease with which she could delve into her unconscious.

But then she was confronted with the heavy metal door, the rust, its age, the sense of its weight. This struck her as heavy emotional stuff, old stuff, stuff she should have cleared out years ago. And yet, the door didn't appear to be locked. All she had to do was open it and walk through.

Instead, she woke up. She thought this indicated that she wasn't ready to confront whatever lay behind the metal door. It puzzled her that there were no other people in the dream. She felt it indicated that the journey into the house was essentially a journey into herself, a journey she had to take alone.

To a Freudian psychologist, this dream could mean that Janet harbors some terrible secret, possibly related to her sexuality, that probably dates back to her childhood. To a Jungian psychologist, the metal door might symbolize beginnings and endings. But the only interpretation that matters is Janet's. This dream, after all, is *her* dream, coughed up from the stew of *her* unconscious, which makes it as personal as personal gets.

Most dream researchers agree that we all can use our dreams as tools for better understanding ourselves, for dealing with and solving our waking-life problems, or even as a way of increasing our creativity and productivity. We can use them to enhance relationships, gain insight about a health problem, obtain career guidance, or even find a new town to live in.

By following the instructions for recalling, recording, and interpreting dreams that are presented throughout the following chapters, you can avoid letting your dreams slip away from you, and gain a new perspective on your life. Even if you already recall and record dreams, you'll discover new ways for interpreting and understanding them. You may also gain new ideas about lucid dreams or out-of-body dreams—that intriguing realm where you are both asleep and awake at the same time. With practice, you can learn how to program dreams and adventure into new worlds, meet both friends and intriguing strangers, and even search past lives and get a peek at future events.

PART ONE

The Dream
Scene

The inventor wrestled for years over one small but vital detail he needed in order to complete a machine he was building. But the detail eluded him. It was like a mirage that vanished whenever he got too close to the answer. Then one night he dreamed he had been taken captive by savages and they were attacking him with spears that had eye-shaped holes at the end. When he woke up, he realized the nightmare had provided the solution to his problem: The eye of the needle belonged near the point! Elias Howe was then able to complete his invention of the sewing machine.

The history of dreams is rich with stories like this—stories that illustrate the incredible fertility of our nightly dreams. Take physicist Neils Bohr. When he dreamed that planets were attached to pieces of string that circled the sun, he was able to develop his theory about the movement of electrons. Albert Einstein literally "dreamed up" his theory of relativity—it came to him while he was dozing. Richard Bach, the author of *Jonathan Livingston Seagull,* dreamed the second half of his book eight years after he'd written the first half. Ingmar Bergman's movie *Cries and Whispers* was inspired by a dream.

The English poet Samuel Taylor Coleridge dozed off one afternoon after taking opium as a sedative. The last words he read before he fell asleep were "Here the Khan Kubla commanded a palace to be built." Coleridge awoke three hours later with between two hundred and three hundred lines of poetry in his head. He quickly wrote the opening lines of Kubla Khan:

> *Our conscious minds are needed if we are to make the most of our dreams; by bringing them into waking consciousness and learning to understand them we may be led to a reappraisal of our whole mode of being.*
>
> —ANN FARADAY,
> *DREAM POWER*

In Xanadu did Kubla Khan
A stately pleasure-dome decree:
Where Alph, the sacred river, ran
Through caverns measureless to man
Down to a sunless sea.

After completing fifty-four lines, Coleridge was interrupted by a visitor. When he returned to his work an hour later, the inspiration had vanished "like images on the surface of a stream." But his masterpiece was complete.

A dream about a snake helped the German chemist Friedrich August Kekule complete his quest to comprehend the molecular structure of the chemical compound benzene.

HOROSCOPE

———————————— ■ ————————————

Do you read your horoscope daily? If you dream your chart is being cast, you will have unexpected changes in your life (of course, you probably will be taking a long journey). You also will be dealing with strangers regarding your business affairs.

If you dream a soothsayer is reading the stars and predicting your future, you will probably find disappointment in life.

If you dream of someone seeing your fortune in a crystal ball, that indicates you are contemplating some complicated events in your life. But use caution. For a young woman to have this dream indicates she is trying to make the best choice between two men!

The atoms, dancing in his dream, suddenly turned into a snake with its tail in its mouth, and when he woke up—"as if struck by lightning"—he realized that the structure he was searching for was shaped like a ring.

Through Time

The ancient Egyptians sought to decipher dreams in terms of prophecy. In a papyrus dream book that dates back nearly fifteen hundred years before the birth of Christ, certain dream symbols are explained. If you dreamed, for example, that your teeth were falling out, it meant your relatives were plotting to kill you.

In ancient Greece, dreams were believed to be conduits to a higher power. People sought curative dreams by sleeping in temples with snakes, which symbolized healing. In the second century A.D., a Greek soothsayer named Artemidorous proved to be so skillful an analyst of dreams that he won Freud's admiration many centuries later. His books on dreams were actually preserved for nearly a thousand years and were still being used when the rationalists came into power.

Renaissance heroes essentially dismissed the importance of dreams. Shakespeare, despite Hamlet's eloquent soliloquy on the nature of dreams, called them "the children of an idle brain." Dryden wrote them off to indigestion and infections of the blood. This bias against dreams persisted into the nineteenth century, when dreams were viewed as

ESP DREAMS

Telepathic and precognitive dreams were explored more fully by Montague Ullman, a New York psychiatrist. In 1953 he designed a dream-telepathy experiment that involved a "sender" and a "receiver."

The receiver, attached by electrodes to an electro-encephalograph, would go to sleep in one room while a sender waited in another room. As soon as the receiver entered the dreaming state, the sender would open an envelope and concentrate on a target picture that had been sealed inside.

In one instance, when Ullman was the sender, his thoughts drifted away from the target picture to the book *Spartacus*. The receiver reported dreaming about the movie *Spartacus*. Results like this convinced Ullman that dream telepathy warranted deeper research.

In 1962 he and Stanley Krippner opened a dream laboratory at Maimonides Medical Center, in Brooklyn, where they expanded their series of dream telepathy experiments. The results were mixed, but the successes were significant enough to convince Ullman that dream telepathy exists.

the end result of an external stimulus. Rain on a rooftop, for example, might trigger a dream about the roof of your house falling in. Beyond the literal translation of the external stimulus, it was believed that dreams held no meaning.

Along came Freud.

Although he was paternalistic and his views today appear excessively fixated on sexual matters, he transformed the way people viewed their dreams. Suddenly, the metaphorical landscapes of our nightly sojourns assumed a personal, internal meaning. In the process, Freud led the way out of the repressive Victorian era when any talk of sex was taboo.

According to Freud, dreams were the expression of forbidden sexual longings that originated in childhood. Like the ancient Greeks, he believed that dreams, once understood, could heal. The main difference between the two, really, was that the Greeks sought physical healing and Freud sought to cure emotional disorders. Although Freud maintained that most dreams were "wish fulfillment" for repressed sexual desires, Carl Jung disagreed with him.

This disagreement eventually led to a falling out between the two psychotherapists. Jung, who began as one of Freud's disciples, thought that sexuality was just one of several themes that appeared in dreams. He argued that dreams didn't *disguise* the unconscious; they *revealed* it. Jung eventu-

ally followed a path that was quite separate and distinct from Freud's.

Jung's research took him into uncharted areas of man's psyche. He theorized the existence of a "collective unconscious," in which all men, regardless of race, religion, or background, are united by a common pool of knowledge and experience that often manifests in dreams.

His exploration of esoteric realms—telepathy, precognition, astrology, the I Ching, tarot, poltergeists, and hauntings—led him to one of his most important theories; he found meaningful patterns in chance events, a phenomenon he referred to as synchronicity. Although such "coincidences" are outside the realm of cause and effect, Jung believed they were the manifestation of an underlying pattern in nature. For Jung, synchronicity served as an explanation for precognition, as exhibited in the following dream.

In his autobiography, *Memories, Dreams, and Reflections,* Jung relates a dream in which he was attending a garden party. His sister was there with a mutual friend from the town of Basel, a woman whom Jung knew well. In the dream, he knew the woman was going to die. But when he woke up, he couldn't remember who the woman was, even though the dream remained vivid in his mind. "A few weeks later, I received news that a friend of mine had a fatal accident. I knew at once that she was the person I had seen in the dream but had been unable to identify."

PARADISE, ADAM & EVE, HELL

Whatever your idea of paradise is—the Garden of Eden; a double-header on a Saturday afternoon; beer and hot dogs; watching MTV all day—just imagine a perfect world and you are in Paradise. If you dream you are in Paradise, it means all your friends are loyal! If you are a mother and dream you are in Paradise, your children will be fair and obedient.

If you dream of Adam and Eve, that famous couple who lived in the traditional Paradise, it means that some event will rob you of success. Remember Adam and Eve weren't exactly the models of success: they got kicked out of Paradise. So beware, and tread softly. If you dream of Adam in a fig leaf and Eve with only a serpent covering her waist and abdomen, treachery and evil will quell your fortune.

If you dream in the other direction—of Hell—beware. If in your dream you are in Hell with the devil, you will fall into temptations that will destroy you and your reputation. If you dream of some of your friends in Hell, you will soon hear of your friends' misfortunes.

9

Lucid Dreaming

Stephen LaBerge, of the Stanford University Sleep Research Center, proved that people can be fully conscious while they're asleep and dreaming. LaBerge claims that lucid dreaming can be taught to virtually anyone and that with a little practice, an individual can be taught to manipulate and control these lucid dreams. By becoming an efficient lucid dreamer, he says, you can overcome deeply rooted fears and anxieties, awaken creativity, and harness the mind's healing power.

Lucid dreaming has figured prominently in the works of Carlos Castaneda. Don Juan, Castaneda's mentor, continually emphasizes the importance of learning to manipulate the environment of this dreamworld. In this state, he claims, ". . . you have power; you can change things; you may find out countless facts; you can control whatever you want."

Dream Work

Once the domain of professional therapy, dream analysis has gone public. Individuals have many tools available now to analyze their own dreams. Besides books on the subject, there are numerous workshops, seminars, and conferences on dreaming. Many are offered through New Age bookstores and community education programs. But dream workshops have also found their way into the mainstream. Even churches and corpora-tions are involved, and there are numerous discussion groups on the Internet.

"People are increasingly interested in becoming fully human," says Blanche Gallagher, a Catholic nun, who runs dream groups each semester at Loyola University's Institute of Pastoral Studies. "The groups are more popular than ever."

Meanwhile, Peter Mudd, director of the C.G. Jung Institute of Chicago, delves into dreams at corporate management seminars. "Most of these managers come in quite skeptical, but go out pleasantly surprised—or even moved—by how their dreams can help them discover a different dimension to the workplace."

Insight

The benefit of the dream research and workshops is the emergence of heightened awareness concerning dreams and their interpretations. By paying attention to the insight provided by your dreams, you can empower yourself. If you learn to remember your dreams and begin to record them, you'll find that certain symbols and patterns are repeated. By studying and analyzing them, you inadvertently embark on a marvelous journey of self-discovery.

CHAPTER TWO

The Nature of Sleep

You spend about a third of your life asleep. That means that in a lifespan of seventy-five years, you sleep the equivalent of twenty-five years. And yet, not until fairly recently did science understand what happens during sleep.

In a typical night, you pass through four distinct phases of sleep. These are distinguished by the frequency of brain waves, eye movements, and muscle tension.

In the first stage, the rhythms of the brain shift from beta, your normal waking consciousness, to alpha, when brain waves oscillate between eight and twelve cycles per second. Your heart and pulse rates, blood pressure, and body temperature drop slightly. Your muscles begin to relax and you experience drifting sensations. Hypnogogic images—surreal scenes that usually concern your last thoughts before turning out the light or some facet of your waking life—may flit through your mind. These hypnogogic images are often vivid and psychedelic. Though brief, the images can be as meaningful and significant as longer dreams in deeper stages of sleep.

> *Why does the eye see a thing more clearly in dreams than the mind while awake?*
>
> —Leonardo da Vinci

In stage two you experience a deepening of the drifting sensation as you fall into a light slumber. The brain wave pattern now registers theta waves, characterized by rapid bursts of brain activity. On an electroencephalogram, these waves appear as spindles and are believed to signify true sleep. Yet, people who are awakened during this phase report they weren't asleep, but were "thinking."

Most of our dreams occur in stage two. If you watch someone sleeping, you can actually see them dream, because their eyes move back and forth beneath their eyelids. This period of rapid eye movement, or REM, usually lasts for several minutes at a time during the second stage.

Twenty to forty-five minutes or so after the sleep cycle begins, the spindle pattern of brain waves is replaced by large, slow delta waves. Delta waves indicate the plunge into deeper stages of slumber. In stage three the EEG consists of 20 to 50 percent delta waves; and in stage four the EEG registers more than 50 percent delta waves. People who are awakened from this phase are usually disoriented and want to go back to sleep. There are no eye movements at all. This is also the stage where sleepwalking may occur. The delta waves can last from a few seconds to an hour.

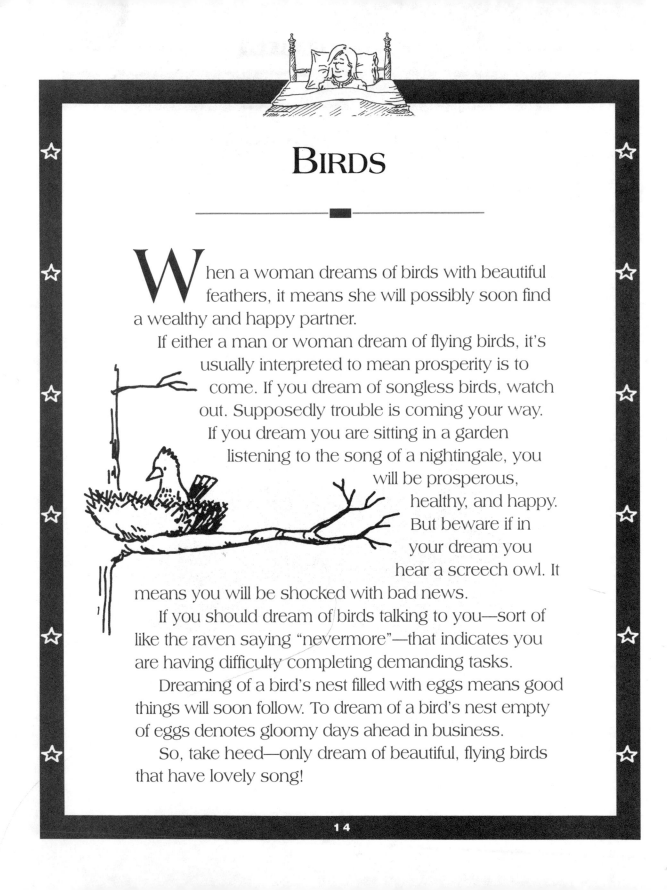

BIRDS

When a woman dreams of birds with beautiful feathers, it means she will possibly soon find a wealthy and happy partner.

If either a man or woman dream of flying birds, it's usually interpreted to mean prosperity is to come. If you dream of songless birds, watch out. Supposedly trouble is coming your way. If you dream you are sitting in a garden listening to the song of a nightingale, you will be prosperous, healthy, and happy. But beware if in your dream you hear a screech owl. It means you will be shocked with bad news.

If you should dream of birds talking to you—sort of like the raven saying "nevermore"—that indicates you are having difficulty completing demanding tasks.

Dreaming of a bird's nest filled with eggs means good things will soon follow. To dream of a bird's nest empty of eggs denotes gloomy days ahead in business.

So, take heed—only dream of beautiful, flying birds that have lovely song!

For example, in an adult male, the cycles of sleep typically last about ninety minutes and then are reversed. But this time, when you reach the second stage again, your blood pressure rises, your pulse quickens, and your brain waves are similar to those during the waking state. Except for twitches in your fingers and toes, and the movement of your eyes in REM sleep, your body becomes virtually paralyzed. If you are awakened during the REM period, you'll probably remember most of whatever you're dreaming.

This first REM period lasts from five to ten minutes, and then you go through the cycles of sleep three or four more times. Each time the REM stage is repeated, it lasts longer and the time that elapses between cycles is considerably shorter. The final REM stage can last as long as an hour.

In practical terms, this means that if you sleep seven hours, then half your dreaming time will occur during the last two hours. If you sleep an additional hour, that eighth hour will consist almost entirely of dreaming. This is, however, only an average. People who need less than eight hours of sleep may simply be more efficient sleepers.

Dreams make up about 20 percent of our sleeping life. In an average lifetime, that means we experience well over a hundred thousand dreams.

Sleep Disturbances

A sleep disturbance doesn't only disrupt your sleep. If you don't sleep well, your dream-time is shortchanged. If you don't dream as you should, you suffer physically, emotionally, and spiritually. It invariably affects the other areas of your life. How you deal with a sleep disturbance is often just as important as the cause of the disturbance.

Mike L. is a former NASA engineer who developed sleep problems while he was working at Cape Canaveral. He was assigned to the 7 a.m. to 3 p.m. shift, which meant he had to get up before 6 a.m. to make it to work. For a morning person, this schedule probably wouldn't be a problem. But Mike is a night owl; his body rhythms lean naturally toward going to bed late and getting up late.

Within a month of working this new schedule, he was worn out from lack of sleep. At the most, he slept a couple of hours a night and was hardly dreaming at all. A coworker suggested he get a prescription for valium or some other sleep aid. But Mike isn't a pill popper and pursued other avenues—warm milk before bedtime, a hot shower, moving his bed, the elimination of caffeine from his diet. But nothing worked.

He continued on this schedule for nearly a year. And then, in January of 1986, the space shuttle Challenger blew up. This event, coupled with what was now a full-blown sleep disturbance, prompted Mike to quit his job.

Mike has never returned to work for NASA. Over the last ten years, he has simplified his life, and found meaningful work that he enjoys at his own pace, following the rhythms of his body. Most mornings, he doesn't get up before 10 a.m.

His sleep disturbance has vanished, and he's dreaming again.

Mike's case may not be extreme. About four million people in this country suffer from insomnia. Aside from the lack of sleep itself, an insomniac is robbed of valuable dreamtime that could provide physical, emotional, and spiritual guidance and solutions.

In the following case, Robert and Steve, who had both recently turned forty, started having sleep difficulties at about the same time. The two men worked out at a gym together several times a week and often talked about their sleep difficulties while working out. Their conditions gradually worsened, affecting their jobs and all aspects of their lives.

Steve went to a psychiatrist, who prescribed a tranquilizer. Robert, a freelance commercial artist, listened to self-hypnosis tapes and sampled herbal remedies. Steve's sleep habits immediately improved. In the gym, he boasted that he could lie down on the floor of the gym and be sound asleep within five minutes. Robert's condition initially persisted and showed only minimal improvement.

But within six months, Robert's sleep patterns were back to normal, except for occasional difficult nights. Steve, meanwhile, still depended on prescription drugs to sleep and was often groggy during the day. He had been known for his vibrant, outgoing attitude, but his friends and associates noticed a personality change. He seemed dull and withdrawn. After more than a year on the drugs, he finally admitted the side effects were worse than the original condition, and began inquiring about natural remedies.

Pregnancy

Even if you have a normal pregnancy, your sleep patterns may change. Early in the last trimester, physical discomforts could awaken you in the middle of the night. Unfortunately, once the baby is born, you will probably get even less sleep.

You can forget about eight hours of uninterrupted, blissful, dream-filled sleep. In fact, you can forget all your notions about what constitutes sleep. Babies, after all, get hungry about every four hours, and they don't care where the food comes from as long as they're fed.

Since you're sleeping less, you're dreaming less, and you're probably recalling fewer dreams. However, some women report particularly vivid dreams during pregnancy, especially during the last trimester. These dreams often have to do with the unborn baby and may express the woman's anxieties over the impending labor and delivery. Women who are open to the concept of telepathic communication with their unborn child may experience dreams in which they're conversing with a small boy or girl.

Age and Sleep

Age is the most important natural factor that influences sleep. A fetus spends as much as 80 percent of its time in the womb in REM sleep. Before the thirtieth week in utero, nearly *all* of its sleep is REM, which is believed to supply intense stimulation to the central nervous system.

It's unknown whether a fetus's REM sleep involves dreaming. Researchers who believe that the contents of dreams are derived from life argue that a fetus can't possibly be dreaming. But in cultures where reincarnation is an accepted belief system, these REM sleep periods in a fetus might be viewed as dreams from a previous life that are somehow preparing the soul for this life.

In the first few weeks after birth, an infant sleeps about sixteen hours a day and may spend as much as eight to ten hours in REM sleep. This is also the time when the baby's brain grows at a staggering rate. The correlation between these two facts is not

Exercise 1: SLEEP HABITS

Use Exercise 1 to track your sleep habits for two weeks. Note the time you went to sleep, approximately how long it took you to go to sleep, the time you woke up, how you felt, whether you were rested, whether you napped in the afternoon, and anything else that pertains to your sleep patterns. This will prepare you for the dream work you'll be doing later in this book.

Sunday

Bedtime: .... Awake Time: ....

Comments: ....

....

Monday

Bedtime: .... Awake Time: ....

Comments: ....

....

Tuesday

Bedtime: .... Awake Time: ....

Comments: ....

....

Wednesday

Bedtime: .... Awake Time: ....

Comments: ....

....

Thursday

Bedtime: .... Awake Time: ....

Comments: ....

....

Friday

Bedtime: .... Awake Time: ....

Comments: ....

....

Saturday

Bedtime: .... Awake Time: ....

Comments: ....

EXERCISE

Sunday

Bedtime: .... Awake Time: ....

Comments: ....

....

Monday

Bedtime: .... Awake Time: ....

Comments: ....

....

Tuesday

Bedtime: .... Awake Time: ....

Comments: ....

....

Wednesday

Bedtime: .... Awake Time: ....

Comments: ....

....

Thursday

Bedtime: .... Awake Time: ....

Comments: ....

....

Friday

Bedtime: .... Awake Time: ....

Comments: ....

....

Saturday

Bedtime: .... Awake Time: ....

Comments: ....

Additional Comments: ....

....

....

random. Some neurophysiologists believe that the internal stimulation of dreams triggers neurological growth in the brain and helps prepare the infant for its waking environment.

By two years of age, the brain of a child has nearly doubled in size. The child is sleeping fewer hours—about thirteen—and is spending less time in REM sleep. By four or five years of age, a child's dream cycles are similar to those of an adult.

If prompted, small children (two to four years of age) will talk about their dreams. In some cultures, where dreams are accorded great respect, this is a regular part of life; and children are encouraged to remember and discuss their dreams.

Brian Weiss, the Miami psychiatrist who wrote the best-selling *Many Lives, Many Masters,* notes that dreams have many functions. "They may provide pathways to recovering repressed or forgotten memories, whether from childhood, infancy, in-utero experiences, or even from past lives."

The Elderly

By the time you're sixty years old, your sleep cycle is more fragmented and variable than it was when you were forty. While the average night's sleep doesn't change all that much, the time spent in deep sleep does. Since the elderly tend to be lighter sleepers, they are awakened more easily during the night.

Insomnia among the elderly is a pervasive problem. But in many instances, it's the result of lying in bed and, like insomniacs of all ages, worrying about the loss of sleep. This behavior also affects the ability to dream.

Your Sleep Requirements

To some extent, your social and cultural expectations have influenced your ideas about how much sleep you're supposed to have. While eight hours is considered to be the average, some people need less and some need more.

If you're one of those fortunate people who feels fine after six hours of sleep, then it simply means you're a more efficient sleeper. You also have two more hours a day at your disposal.

In general, you may need less sleep when your life is humming along on an even keel. During periods of illness, stress, depression, pregnancy, or tumultuous change, you may need more sleep.

CHAPTER THREE

Fantastic Dreams and Dreamers

Everyone is a dream traveler, even people who don't recall their dreams. But some individuals explore their dreams in depth, and their discoveries have added immeasurably to our knowledge of dreams. Here are the stories of a few of those dreamers and their contributions.

The Sleeping Prophet

Most of us go to sleep at night, surrender to our dreams, then wake up in the morning and get on with our lives. We may or may not mull over our dreams, or explore their symbolism, their tales. It's our choice. But for a grade-school dropout from Kentucky, the dreams and visions that rose from sleep *were* his life.

Edgar Cayce (1877-1945) has been called the greatest seer of the twentieth century. And yet, he was never on television, never sought publicity, and never wrote a best-selling book. However, for much of his sixty-seven years, Edgar Cayce did extraordinary things in his sleep. He diagnosed illnesses

> *The dream is the small hidden door in the deepest and most intimate sanctum of the soul.*
>
> — CARL GUSTAV JUNG

with astonishing accuracy and recommended treatments that for his time were unorthodox, but that have gained enormous support in the years since his death. With nothing more than a person's name and geographical location, he could give a detailed description of an individual's physical condition and then prescribe certain therapies about which he knew nothing in his waking life.

Cayce also gave "life readings" for many of the people who consulted him for medical advice. These readings covered a vast spectrum of topics from spiritual matters to love and relationships to business, past lives, prophecies, and dreams. More than fourteen thousand of Cayce's readings are preserved at the Association for Research and Enlightenment in Virginia Beach. Of these, over a thousand deal with dreaming.

Cayce, like Jung, believed that many dreams hold a psychic content. Both dreamed presciently of their own deaths. Both dreamed about the rise of Hitler and the beginning of World War II long before it happened. But even more importantly, both of these men, contemporaries separated by half a world and totally different views of life, believed that our dreams are our most personal sources of self-knowledge.

"Any condition is first dreamed before it becomes reality," Cayce said.

Cayce, like Jung, believed that dream symbols are highly individualistic, that each of us stamps common symbols according to our own perceptions and worldviews. And yet, through the readings that Cayce gave on symbols, certain common meanings emerge:

☆ *Animals:* represent man's negative and positive qualities (the wilder the animal, the more primitive the emotion).

☆ *A Boat:* life's voyage.

☆ *Fire:* a cleansing, wrath, or destruction.

☆ *Fish:* Christ, spirituality, spiritual journey, or spiritual forces.

☆ *Fishing:* man's search for higher consciousness.

☆ *A House:* the body, the self.

☆ *Mandalas:* reveal the inner state of the dreamer, a thrust for wholeness.

☆ *Mud or tangled weeds:* need for cleansing, for purification.

☆ *Naked image:* exposure or feeling vulnerable to the criticism of others.

☆ *Snake:* wisdom or sex or both.

☆ *Water:* the unconscious, the source of life, or a spiritual journey.

Cayce believed that dreams fell under four general headings: problems with the physical body, self-observation, psychic perception, and spiritual guidance. Jung's breakdown is more complex, a reflection of his slant as a psychologist, but there are striking similarities in their beliefs about dreams and what they mean. In the list, the definitions that are starred are ones on which Cayce and Jung agreed.

Although the two men never discussed the meaning of dream symbols, they may very well have obtained the meanings from the same source. Cayce called it "the universal mind," and Jung termed it "the collective unconscious."

Joy's Way

Personal transformation is rarely the same for any two people. But sometimes a physical threat serves as the catalyst that sets the entire process in motion.

For William Brugh Joy, a life-threatening disease (chronic relapsing pancreatitis) in 1974 prompted him to abandon a thriving medical practice in Los Angeles. Within six weeks, his pancreatitis was cured and he was embarked on a transformative journey that, twenty-two years later, is still unfolding. Dreams have been and are an intricate part of his journey.

A dream, in fact, was the trigger for Joy writing his first book, *Joy's Way*. In the dream, he was signing his medical chart and noticed that it was disorganized. He straightened out the chart, then realized the signature was odd. It was written last name first, as it would appear on a death certificate. To the right of his name was an asterisk and a

note that directed him to "see box above." Written in the box, in red pencil and capital letters, were the words *PLEASE HURRY!*

To Joy, the significance of the dream was obvious. He needed to organize the transformational material he used with groups, in order to clarify and summarize it. In a sense, the book would serve as a closure to the first part of his journey. The eleven-chapter outline popped into his head as he was falling asleep one afternoon. He simultaneously heard a voice that ordered him to get up and write down the organization of the book.

So he did.

In his transformational workshops and conferences, Joy emphasizes dream interpretation. He stresses that the goal isn't merely to understand one particular dream or another, but to achieve self-insight so that you can continue to interpret your dreams in the future. In this way, he is similar to both Jung and Cayce.

But whereas both Jung and Cayce seemed to accept certain symbols as gospel, Joy believes there is never an absolute meaning for any dream symbol. He points out that water in one dream may represent the unconscious, but in another it may symbolize emotions. "The best dream analysts are intuitive, and so are the best dream analyses."

When you hit on the correct interpretation of a dream, Joy says, you feel a "zing," a sensation that you're in tune with what the dream was communicating. Jung referred to this phenomenon as a "click." In both cases, it's an intuitive sense, a hunch that you're on the right track.

With his own dreams, Joy uses seven different perspectives for interpretation:

1. Physical
2. Sexual
3. Emotional
4. Collective human viewpoint
5. Higher creative viewpoint
6. Mental
7. Universal

One of the techniques that Joy advocates is the use of tarot cards in the interpretation of dreams. "The Tarot operates primarily through the symbolic, nonrational aspects of consciousness, the same state from which dreams communicate."

When you shuffle and lay out the cards in a particular spread, it's as if you're presented with a dream. Both are mosaics that form a pattern and the patterns are what you interpret. Joy, in his second book, *Avalanche*, calls these mosaics "pattern projections." They are evident in astrology and numerology and, according to Joy, are also evident in odd places like clouds. He believes the deeper levels of the mind "can project onto the clouds a pattern that is germane to a question that has been posed."

By learning to read patterns in this way, it becomes easier to interpret your own dreams.

Through dream interpretation, you open channels to the deeper parts of your mind

and begin to perceive yourself and your life in entirely new ways. Once you're aware of these patterns, they sometimes manifest when you're awake. Joy cites a startling example from his own life, which happened in Hawaii.

He and a young woman, who recently had had a mastectomy, were talking about angels. Although her prognosis was excellent, Joy sensed that she was orienting herself toward death. As they talked, a lone seagull swept past them, then flew straight up into the air and vanished. At that moment, Joy knew with utter certainty that the woman would die very soon.

"An omen had been delivered through the very unusual flight pattern of the seagull. I cannot describe the extent to which this process is disturbing to my intellect or how the process actually works . . ."

The woman died within a year.

In a sense, these external patterns are analogous to the waking dream symbols discussed earlier. At some point in your dream explorations, the things you learn begin to spill over into your waking life. This fact seems to be true for most people who commit to the journey.

Seth Meets Jane Roberts

One evening in 1963, Jane Roberts and her husband, Robert Butts, experimented with a Ouija board. Their simple experiment altered the course of their lives.

Almost immediately, a "personality essence" who called himself Seth began spelling out messages on the board. The information was so evocative, Butts wrote down the material and they decided to continue their experiment.

By the third or fourth session, Roberts began to hear the messages in her head as they were being spelled out. She and her husband dispensed with the Ouija board and from that point on, Roberts spent a good deal of the next three decades in trance, channeling Seth.

This strange collaboration produced ten books that were channeled by Seth and more than a dozen published books that Roberts wrote, based on the Seth concepts. These ideas, which Seth referred to as "psychic constructs," became the cornerstone of the couple's spiritual journey. Not surprisingly, dreams played a major role in this journey.

The basis of the Seth material is astonishingly simple: You literally create your reality through your beliefs. But when you really think about what this statement implies, you realize its complexity. Exactly what *are* your beliefs? Which beliefs are visible? Which are invisible? How are these beliefs formed and how can you change them? The answer, says Seth, is through dreams.

"All of your grandest civilizations have existed first in the world of dreams," Seth remarked during a session in 1979. "You might say that the universe dreamed itself into being . . . All worlds have an inner beginning."

PROFANITY & BLASPHEMY

— ■ —

Did your parents tell you that when you used profanity and blasphemy you were turning into a coarse person? Well, if you dream of swearing or blasphemy it denotes that you are cultivating coarse traits. If you dream others are blasting you with profanity, you are in for some rough times.

Just for the record, profanity means not respecting that what is holy. Blasphemy is more specific—it means taking God's name in vain.

Vice, on the other hand, are actions you take that harm others. If you dream of harming others, by deceit, telling lies, or injuring their reputation in some way, it denotes that your reputation is about to plummet.

This comment bears an uncanny parallel to one of Cayce's: "Any condition is first dreamed before it becomes reality."

Seth contends that dreams possess their own reality, that in a very literal sense they are as "real" as the waking world. The only difference is that they don't adhere to the same laws. In *The Unknown Reality,* he says, "From the other side—within what is loosely called the dream state—there is an existence quite as valid as your own, and from that viewpoint *you can be considered the dreamer.*"

From these dream states, you take "snapshots" of probable actions and situations that you want to manifest into physical existence. Dreams are the place where you "sample" actions, relationships, situations, everything that makes up physical existence. From this, you select experiences that become your physical reality.

Dreams, according to Seth, acquaint you with the reality that exists after death. The more capable you are in recalling and exploring your dreams, the more familiar you will be with the afterlife state. "In the dream state you learn, among other things, how to construct your own physical reality day by day, just as after death you learn how to construct your next physical lifetime."

When Roberts began her exploration, she often grappled with the meanings of her dreams. The dreams themselves seemed to be chaotic, senseless, without any discernible pattern. But as she worked with her dreams, as she studied them, she noticed that her dream activities really weren't chaotic; they simply possessed a different type of order than events in her waking life. She came to believe that dreams have a continuity, a history, just as waking life does.

Roberts learned to shift her focus: Instead of contemplating the world around her, she used her environment as a window into herself. It's as if she stepped to one side of normal time and events, aware of them, but centered her concentration elsewhere.

This kind of shift in focus probably happens more often than you realize. You might be walking on a beach at sunset, for instance, your attention riveted on the shells around you, when you glance up at the setting sun. The sight of it sweeps you into a different sort of awareness and you suddenly "see" a figure composed of light dancing on the surface of the ocean.

This figure, according to Roberts's view, would be every bit as real as the warm sand under your feet. But because it isn't part of "consensus reality," of society's recognized order of things, you dismiss it.

In October 1974, shortly after Roberts and her husband had moved into the house she occupied until her death, she was sitting at her desk when she suddenly saw a library superimposed over the far corner of the room. She had inadvertently shifted her focus so that she could perceive it and realized this library was connected to the next book she would write.

Not long afterward, she began to dream about the library and found that she had access to the information contained in its collection. In a sense, it was as if she were bringing its information into the waking world through her books.

If she had denied the reality of that initial experience simply because it didn't fit into "consensus reality," she might have closed off a rich source for future books and an entire dream area that furthered her spiritual growth. The same can be said of her and her husband's initial experience with the Ouija board. If they had been less adventurous, the Seth material might not have manifested in the world as we know it.

Judith Orloff

In Western culture, psychiatrists do not profess to be psychic, even if they are, because they risk ridicule and open themselves to accusations that they are mentally deranged. But Judith Orloff, a Los Angeles psychiatrist, did exactly that when she wrote *Second Sight*.

Dreams have always been integral to Orloff's life. "Dreams are my compass and my truth; they guide me and link me to the divine." As a child, when her mother cautioned her not to talk about her predictions, dreams comforted her. As a rebellious teen, her dreams perplexed her. As a young adult, her dreams seemed to guide her, nudging her in particular directions.

Her earliest remembered dream, which she recalled under hypnotic regression as an adult, occurred while she was still in the womb, when her mother was five months pregnant. Fibroid tumors had grown on the outside of her mother's uterus and were pressing inward. She remembered hearing the noises of the surgery and waking in a dark, watery, alien place. She tried desperately to return home, but didn't have any idea where home was.

She began to dream of a small farmhouse. A blond woman, the woman's husband, and their two teenage sons came out to greet her. Orloff felt an immediate kinship with them, as though they were her real family. This same family, she said, kept her company until she was born.

Orloff, like Roberts, believes each of us has a "dream history." By tracing this history, regardless of how far back the dream goes, it's possible to fill in gaps in your life. This missing information often allows you to illuminate hidden memories that explain who you are.

She classifies dreams into two distinct types: psychological and psychic, with various subcategories under each type. The majority of dreams, she says, fall under the first category.

In psychological dreams, anxieties, fears, and insecurities sometimes surface. They may come in the form of nightmares or simply as unpleasant dreams. Also under this category are guidance dreams, or dreams in which you are advised on a particular course or solution to a problem.

Orloff cites a guidance dream she had about a problem with a colleague, in which she was clearly cautioned to wait a few days

Notes

Use this section for any questions or ideas that crop up as you read through part one.

before confronting the man. Despite the clarity of the message, she started to call his beeper, then changed her mind and phoned a friend first.

Her friend related a dream she'd had the night before about Orloff, in which they were sitting in a room with their meditation teacher. The teacher turned to her friend and told her to tell Orloff not to do anything right now, that she should allow some time to pass. Orloff was so struck by the message that she allowed several days to go by before confronting her colleague.

When you're analyzing a guidance dream, there are specific clues to look for. Orloff, like Joy, refers to the "zing" of recognition, something that grabs your attention.

It might be a word or phrase or a particular image. Listen to your body's responses. A chill, goose bumps, or a sudden hollowness in the pit of your stomach are all indications that the dream has hit on an answer you need.

There are two kinds of psychic dreams: precognitive and healing. In precognitive dreams, the focus is on some future event that may or may not involve you personally. In healing dreams, you may receive guidance about how to deal with a physical problem or you may experience what seems to be a

metaphorical healing, though it actually affects you physically.

Carl Jung

Born in Switzerland toward the end of the 1800s, Carl Gustav Jung is probably better known now, more than thirty years after his death, than he was during his lifetime.

Many of his discoveries about the unconscious came to him initially through dreams, which were his richest source of information, his conduit to the deeper mysteries he studied for most of his life. His theories on the collective unconscious, archetypes, synchronicity, and dream interpretation essentially redefined psychology—deepening it—and made it accessible to ordinary people.

There are many references to Jung throughout this book, a tribute to his enormous creativity and the range of his research. Jung, like the other dreamers cited in this chapter, understood that dreaming is an ancient art, to some extent a lost art, one that begs to be revived. The first step to reviving that art begins in part two, with remembering your dreams.

PART TWO

Dream
Techniques

CHAPTER FOUR

Remembering Dreams

Sometimes, dreams are so startling or vivid that you come awake during the night.

At that time, you might think, *I won't forget this one.* Yet, by morning a fog may settle over your memories of the night's "events" and you may only recall the flavor of the dream and little else. Or, you may just remember thinking that you weren't going to forget your dream.

The best way to remember dreams is to record them immediately after they occur. If you don't usually wake up after a dream, try giving yourself a suggestion before you go to sleep that you will wake up following each dream, although it might not be a good idea to do so every night. You may reach a point where you can recall four or five or more dreams a night.

Either jot down the dream on a bedside pad or record it on a tape. If you decide to write down the dream, you can either use a penlight or learn to write in the dark. At first, your night-time scrawls may be virtually indecipherable, but with practice you can write clearly enough so that you will be able to transcribe the dream into a journal in the morning.

> *To catch your dream, have pen and paper or a tape recorder by your bed—a material suggestion.*
>
> — SHEILA OSTRANDER AND LYNN SCHROEDER

The next best time to recall a dream is in the morning before you get up. The experts all seem to agree that how you awaken in the morning is vital to preliminary recall of dreams. If you can dispense with an alarm clock, by all means do so. An alarm intrudes, jerking you from a sound sleep so quickly that your dream tends to fade as soon as you open your eyes.

To awaken without an alarm, of course, is difficult if you're working a nine-to-five job or have young children. One alternative is to start your dream work on a weekend, when you may be able to sleep later and to wake up without an alarm. Another alternative is to train yourself to wake up without an alarm. This is actually much easier to do than it sounds. Before going to sleep at night, simply give yourself a suggestion to wake up at a particular time, say, ten minutes before your alarm clock goes off. If it doesn't work immediately, keep trying until you feel confident you can eliminate the alarm clock.

Once you wake up, don't open your eyes. Just lie there for a few minutes, retrieving your dream images. If nothing comes to mind, move into your favorite sleep position. This may trigger some dream fragment that will expand.

"For some as yet unknown reason," writes Patricia Garfield in her book *Creative Dreaming,* "additional dream recall often comes when you move gently from one position and settle into another."

At first, you may remember only bits and pieces, an image, a word, a face. But with practice, large parts of your last dream will come to you. These parts, in turn, may trigger a memory of the dream before it. Eventually, this process will become automatic, as intrinsic to your morning ritual as brushing your teeth.

Sometimes it helps to have reference points to aid you in the recollection of a dream.

Quite often, our own thoughts about our dreams are the biggest obstacles to recalling

GIVING YOURSELF A SUGGESTION TO REMEMBER YOUR DREAMS

The best suggestions occur in a slightly altered state, when your mind is more open.

In the twilight state as you drift to sleep at night, tell yourself that you will recall the most important dream you dream that night. If you have a specific question that you want answered, tell yourself that you'll remember the dream that answers that question.

Repeat this request several times as you fall asleep. Make sure that your journal and a pen are within reach.

Since most of our dreaming occurs in the early morning hours, this is an excellent time to give yourself a suggestion. Set your alarm thirty or forty minutes earlier than you usually get up. Put it in the music mode, so you awaken more gently.

When the alarm goes off, try not to open your eyes. Lie there quietly for a few minutes and tell yourself you're going to fall back to sleep and have an important dream—or a dream that answers a particular question. Strongly urge yourself to recall the dream.

In quiet moments throughout the day, tell yourself that tonight you're going to remember your dreams. If you have particular questions you want answered, phrase those questions to yourself. Sometimes, you only need to repeat your intention several times through a day, like an affirmation. Tonight I remember my dreams. Or: Tonight I get answers through my dreams.

Experiment with different methods until you find the one that works best for you. It helps if you sincerely believe you can receive answers through your dreams.

them. A dream may be so unusual that you wake up certain that you'll remember it, only to forget it within minutes of opening your eyes. On the other hand, you might think a dream is too silly or embarrassing to write down, or that it's not worth remembering.

It's best to avoid making value judgments about a dream and simply write it down as if it were someone else's story. Later, when you interpret the dream, you may find that what seemed silly or outrageous or insignificant has far deeper meaning than you initially realized.

The Dream Journal

A dream journal is an integral part of dream exploration, a portal to other parts of yourself that is rather like the hole Alice fell through on her way to Wonderland. A notebook will do, but a bound journal is even better. Many bookstores now sell bound journals with blank pages inside. Some are specifically designed as dream journals and include a place for the date and time of the dream, the dream itself, and your interpretation.

If your bedside writing isn't clear, transcribe your dreams later into a "permanent" notebook or onto a computer file. If you use a notebook computer, keep it near the bed and type the dreams directly into it when you wake up.

Keep the journal and a penlight nearby—on a nightstand, on the floor, or even under your pillow. If you jot down your dreams during the

night or tape record them, then set aside a time to transcribe them into your journal.

When you describe the dream, include as many details as possible. The interrogatives—*who, what, where, when, and how*—act as excellent guidelines in collecting details. Were you alone? If not, who was with you? Friends? Family? Strangers? What activity, if any, were you or the others engaged in? Was it day or night? Dark or light? Where were you? How did the dream "feel" to you? Familiar? Odd? Pleasant?

Brugh Joy attributes particular significance to the lighting in a dream. If a dream is brilliantly colored and very vivid, it reflects what he calls the "superconscious" state, the more evolved areas of consciousness. In his own life, these types of dreams are nearly always prophetic. If the light in a dream is soft or shadowy, in sepia tones like an old photograph, or if it's in black and white, Joy says it emanates from less evolved areas of consciousness. Dreams that are even darker originate from the deep unconscious. When you record a dream, one of the details that should be included is how you felt upon awakening. What is your dominant emotion? Exhilaration? Fear? Sadness? Happiness? Sometimes, when you go over the dream later, you may remember more details.

Montague Ullman advises that when you record a dream, jot down whatever you were thinking about when you went to bed. It may provide a clue to the meaning of the dream.

Sometimes, you may not remember the specifics of a dream, but only that you've

Exercise 2: RECALLING A DREAM

This provides a list of points to look for in recalling a dream.

1. What was the location of the dream? ....

   Was it indoors or outdoors? Above ground or below ground? ....
   Was it located in a familiar or an unfamiliar place? Was it located in another
   town or city? ....

2. Were there people involved? ....
   Did you know them or were they strangers? ....
   Were they in your life now or from your past? ....
   Were any of them celebrities? ....

3. What emotions were involved? ....
   Were you exhilarated, happy, afraid, depressed, confused, or lonely? ....

   Did your emotional state change during the dream?
   If so, what caused the change? ....

4. Were there any animals in the dream? ....
   Were they friendly, fierce looking, gentle, or wise? ....

5. What objects or symbols were involved in the dream? ....

6. What was said in the dream? ....

   Did anyone in the dream speak directly to you? What was said? ....

7. What was the major action in the dream? ....

dreamed. Then, later that day or several days later, your recollection of the dream is triggered by something in your waking environment. Be sure to note the event or experience that triggered the recollection, because it may provide vital clues about the dream's meaning or significance.

If you're not getting enough sleep, recalling your dreams is going to be much more difficult. Refer to the exercise in chapter 2 on sleep habits to refresh your memory about how much sleep you need and readjust your schedule accordingly. You may want to note in your journal how long you sleep on a given night and how many times you wake up. If you habitually wake up at night, try taking advantage of the situation by seeing if you can recall any dreams. If you do, then record them. If you initially have trouble recalling dreams at night, then try recapturing a dream when you wake up from a nap. This works well for some people.

Meditation and Dream Recall

Meditation can be another means to help you recall dreams. The process makes you aware of other states of mind, and ultimately may enhance your recollection of dreams. By quieting your conscious mind, symbols and images are allowed to flow more freely from the intuitive self.

The technique you use depends entirely on what feels most natural to you. A walk in the woods or on the beach can serve your purpose just as well as ten or twenty minutes of sitting quietly after you wake up. Orloff meditates every morning in front of an altar that contains objects that hold special meaning for her. When she misses a day, she says, she feels less centered. Brugh Joy rises at 4 a.m. every morning and meditates for an hour.

Another Perspective

The obvious preliminary step in dream work is remembering your dreams. It sounds simple—pen and paper or a recorder nearby, a sincere intent, and suggestions before you fall asleep to recall your dreams. But as Seth—the "personality essence" that Jane Roberts channeled—points out, some people try and try and just can't remember.

In such instances, the problem may lie in an "invisible belief." Perhaps, in your heart of hearts, you're afraid to remember your dreams. Or you're afraid to know what you dream about. Or maybe you believe your dreams may tell you more than you want to know. By examining your beliefs honestly, Seth advises, you'll uncover the invisible or core belief that is preventing you from remembering your dreams.

"You must change your ideas about dreaming, alter your concepts about it, before you can begin to explore it.

HOW TO ENTER A MEDITATIVE STATE:

Begin by meditating five minutes a day, preferably in the morning.

Choose a spot where you won't be interrupted and distractions are minimal.

Sit on the floor in a cross-legged position or, if that's uncomfortable, in a chair. Make sure your back is straight, both feet are on the floor, and you aren't wearing shoes or constrictive clothing.

Start by firmly stating your intent: to remember a dream or expand on one that you recall only in fragments.

Take several long, slow breaths through your nostrils. Watch your breath and let go of your thoughts. (Brugh Joy recommends inhaling slowly through the nostrils, holding your breath, without tension, to the count of seven, and then slowly exhaling through your mouth, with the tip of your tongue touching the roof of your mouth. Then start over again, for a total of ten breaths. Edgar Cayce entered a meditative state through alternate nostril breathing, inhaling through one nostril and exhaling through the other, repeating this several times, and then changing nostrils. However you choose to breathe, be aware of each inhalation as energy.)

Relax your body, starting either with the top of your head or with your toes and feeling all the tension being released from each part.

Quiet your mind by turning off the internal dialogue. Whenever you start thinking, gently release your thoughts and return to the meditative state. Wait for an image or impression to come to mind. This will feel different than a thought. You'll have a sense that it's a message from "elsewhere," a higher part of your self.

Alternately, visualize yourself descending stairs or an elevator, then going to a private movie theatre. Focus on the screen, letting go of all other thoughts. Soon an image may appear related to your concern.

Don't meditate while lying in bed; you may fall asleep.

Meditate on an empty or nearly empty stomach.

Once you're able to meditate for five minutes, expand your time to fifteen or twenty. But don't feel you have to stick to a particular time limit. You are likely to find that by meditating for the purpose of dream recall you will feel more relaxed and centered, and that recalling dreams will be easier. If you continue to have trouble recalling dreams, you might pose a question to yourself before meditating as to why you're experiencing the difficulty.

Otherwise, your own waking prejudice will close the door," says Seth.

Sometimes, you have to recall an image from a dream to remember that you dreamed at all, and what you remember may not make any sense. But other times, the moment you become conscious, the dream is there, smack in front of you, and you capture it in full detail. Most of the time, however, at least until you become proficient in dream recall, you remember piecemeal.

Even so, the benefits of dreaming are never lost, regardless of whether you remember them. Your dreams, says Seth, ". . . constantly alter the chemical balances within your body. A dream may be purposely experienced to provide an outlet of a kind that is missing in your daily life."

In *The Unknown Reality,* Seth outlines a specific way to familiarize yourself with dream landscapes:

1. Before you fall asleep, imagine that you have a dream camera with you.

2. Give yourself the suggestion that you'll take a dream snapshot of the most significant dream of the night.

3. Keep at it; practice.

4. Once you begin to obtain results, write out a description of each scene you remember. Include descriptions of how you felt at the time of the dream, and how you feel as you record it.

5. Note the weather conditions in the dream. Is it raining? Is the sun shining? Is there a pervasive gloom? These weather conditions will tell you a great deal about the inner state of your psyche.

The camera, then, becomes a cue to your inner self that you are serious about dream exploration. By using it in your dream exploration, you will become more aware of these interior landscapes. ". . . Your dream snapshots will show you the kind of experience you are choosing from inner reality."

CELLAR

If you dream you are in a cold, damp cellar, it denotes you will soon be oppressed by doubts. But if you dream you are in a wine cellar, good news. You will share in profits although the profits could come from a doubtful source. If you dream you are in a wine cellar drinking wine—watch out—you might wake up in the morning with a hangover.

If you dream you are in a basement, your pleasure and prosperous possibilities might lesson and even develop into trouble.

If, on the other hand, you dream of the top of a house—a garret—good times are coming your way. If you dream you are climbing stairs to a garret, that dream is telling you that you tend to dwell in theories of life and leave the everyday realities to others. Perhaps you should think about changing your ways.

Exercise 3: DREAM JOURNAL

Here is a sample page from a dream journal. Use this merely as a starting point and feel free to add to it and change it as you like. The beauty of dream work is that it's an empirical process, and we are all pioneers. Use these following pages for one full week and see if there is a difference in the way you remember your dreams.

Date: .... **Time:** ....

Presleep thoughts: ....

....

....

Dream: ....

....

....

Interpretation: ....

....

....

Feelings upon waking: ....

Additional comments: ....

....

....

....

Date: .... **Time:** ....

Presleep thoughts: ....

....

....

Dream: ....

....

....

Interpretation: ....

....

....

Feelings upon waking: ....

....

Additional comments: ....

....

....

....

EXERCISE

Date: .... **Time:** ....

Presleep thoughts: ....

....

....

Dream: ....

....

....

Interpretation: ....

....

....

Feelings upon waking: ....

....

Additional comments: ....

....

....

....

Date: .... **Time:** ....

Presleep thoughts: ....

....

Dream: ....

....

....

Interpretation: ....

....

Feelings upon waking: ....

....

....

Additional comments: ....

....

....

....

Date: .... **Time:** ....

Presleep thoughts: ....

....

....

Dream: ....

....

....

Interpretation: ....

....

....

Feelings upon waking: ....

....

....

Additional comments: ....

....

....

....

Date: .... **Time:** ....

Presleep thoughts: ....

....

....

Dream: ....

....

Interpretation: ....

....

Feelings upon waking: ....

....

Additional comments: ....

....

....

....

Date: .... **Time:** ....

Presleep thoughts: ....

....

Dream: ....

....

Interpretation: ....

....

Feelings upon waking: ....

....

Additional comments: ....

....

....

....

Date: .... **Time:** ....

Presleep thoughts: ....

....

Dream: ....

....

Interpretation: ....

....

Feelings upon waking: ....

....

Additional comments: ....

....

....

....

Let's assume that you are now recalling your dreams, recording them in your journal, and remarking on your feelings about the dreams. But you're often not sure about their meanings.

Sometimes, dream dictionaries help by providing hints at the meaning of symbols that appear in your dreams. But other times, especially when the elements of the dream are personal, the meanings don't resonate for you. No dream dictionary is going to tell you the meaning of a dream about your Uncle Bill, whom you haven't seen for twelve years. So what do you do?

> *All dreams are given for the benefit of the individual, would he but interpret them correctly.*
>
> — EDGAR CAYCE

Metaphors and Puns

Watch for metaphors and puns in your dreams. When you recognize a metaphor, a perplexing dream can take on meaning. When you dream of people who are not in your life anymore, think about what they represent. If Bert from the old job was a gossip, his appearance in a dream might refer to gossip.

The same may be true of dreams about celebrities. For example, a dream of Bob Hope bouncing along on a pogo stick and moving off into the distance might at first seem outrageous and nonsensical. But by looking at the elements of the dream in terms of a play on words, the message is revealed: Hope springs eternal.

A woman who had been reading tarot cards before going to bed saw herself in one dream at a turnstile in a subway station. The token she put in didn't work. A hand reached into her vision and held out a vividly colored tarot card—Strength—which she inserted into a slot. The turnstile began to move and she passed through.

The turnstile, she felt, was a metaphor indicating that she was about to undergo a *turn* or change in her *style* of doing certain things. The Strength card suggested that she possessed the inner resources to make the change successfully.

Archetypes: From Myths to Movies

An archetype is a symbol or theme that rises from a layer of the mind common to

JEWELS

Jewels—precious gems—make the best gifts. Dreaming of jewels, in general, signifies good luck to come. If you dream of owning diamonds, you will have great honor bestowed on you—great honor from high places. Women dreaming of receiving a diamond or diamonds from a lover denotes they will make a great marriage and be happy and wealthy. If you dream you lose a diamond, however, look out for disgrace and need.

If you dream of owning pearls, you will have success in business and be highly regarded in society. If a woman dreams she receives pearls from a lover, she should be prepared for festive occasions. It also denotes she will select a faithful and loving husband. If you dream of a string of pearls breaking, watch out for suffering, sadness, and sorrow.

A dream about a ruby means that your speculation in love or business will turn out well. If you dream of losing a ruby however, your lover will soon be indifferent to you.

To dream of owning emeralds means you will inherit property. Dreaming of a sapphire denotes continuous good fortune. For a woman to dream of emeralds means she will soon make a smart choice in selecting a husband.

all people. Carl Jung called this layer the "collective unconscious" and believed that we each give these symbols and themes our own individual stamp.

Archetypes are prevalent in mythology, folklore, and religion. The hero, for instance, is a common theme in mythology.

From Apollo to Zeus, King Arthur to Luke Skywalker, the hero follows a standard pattern. First, he is cut off from his roots—what mythologist Joseph Campbell terms his *call to adventure.* For Luke Skywalker, this happens with the murder of his aunt and uncle. For ET, the starting point occurs when he is stranded on Earth.

Then the hero sets out on a journey of self-discovery, a rite of passage in which he must confront and overcome villains, disasters, and challenges, to awaken a power within himself. For Luke, this awakening is his contact with "The Force"; for ET, the awakening is trusting the boy who befriends him.

In the *Wizard of Oz,* Dorothy is cut off from her roots by the tornado that whisks her to Oz. On the yellow brick road, she encounters tricksters, witches, and innumerable challenges. She overcomes her fears when she accepts the friendship of her traveling companions—the scarecrow, the tin man, and the cowardly lion—who are on their own heroic journey.

The hero, of course, always reaches his goal. Skywalker saves the world from Darth Vader's evil empire and discovers his true heritage. ET calls home. Dorothy reaches the wizard. But the goal isn't the end of the journey; the hero must return to his ordinary life with his new wisdom and enrich the lives of everyone around him.

You may not consciously recognize an archetype when you encounter it; but it will resonate at some level inside of you. Jung called this sensation a "click," a feeling of rightness.

In the following dream, the archetypal figure literally jumps out at the dreamer.

GARGOYLES

I walk into a room with four doors and a raised platform in the middle with a gargoylelike devil in the middle of the platform. The room is illuminated in light. I don't feel afraid. I walk around the room, closing three of the doors, then walk out the fourth door and shut it behind me. Now I'm in a room filled with smaller gargoylelike creatures. Suddenly, they begin to transform into human beings. I look back at the large gargoyle in the other room and he too is transforming into human form.

Vicki, a librarian, had been going through changes in her life when she dreamed of the gargoyles. She was in the process of leaving behind her old self, which she described as a typical bland Iowa school marm. The new Vicki was discovering other parts of her personality, going

deeper into areas of her personality that she had previously feared. The dream made sense to her and was easy to interpret.

The platform in the room was an altar, and the gargoyle was the devil, the darker elements of her personality. The fact that the room was brightly lit was significant to her. In order to become a whole person, she was illuminating her dark side. The fact that the gargoyles changed into humans signified that we all have a dark side that needs illuminating.

Can you find the archetype in the following dream?

★   ★   ★

SNAKES

I'm walking in tall grass, grass that brushes my knees. I hear rustling around me and pick up my pace, anxious to get to the clearing I can see just ahead. I know the rustling is caused by snakes.

The rustling gets louder, like the cacophony of a thousand crickets screaming for rain. I start running. I'm still running when I reach the clearing and run right into a bed of snakes. They are everywhere, writhing, slithering, rattling. But even worse than the snakes is the realization that I'm barefoot and that the only way I'm going to get out of this is to walk through them.

So I walk. And I make it through the bed of snakes without getting bitten.

★   ★   ★

In the ancient Greek and Roman cultures, snakes were symbols of the healing arts. In the Bible, the snake symbolizes temptation and forbidden knowledge. In fairy tales, the snake is often a trickster, wise but wily. The ancient symbol of the snake swallowing its own tail represents the way nature feeds on and renews itself. Jung considered snakes to be archetypal, representing an awareness of the essential energy of life and nature.

The woman who had this dream was breaking away from a Catholic background to explore areas that the religion of her childhood would call heretical. She interpreted the dream to mean that the prospect of this exploration was somewhat frightening for her, but that she would complete it without "harm." She felt the dream was confirming her belief that the exploration was a necessary step in her growth as a human being.

On another level, though, she felt the dream was pointing to a situation at work, one in which she was surrounded by "snakes in the grass"—a pun that probably indicated malicious gossip. But since the snakes didn't bite her, she figured she would survive whatever was being said about her.

Even though the snake is considered an archetypal symbol, in this case the meaning that was most relevant to the dreamer concerned her daily life. She didn't need a psychologist to interpret the dream for her; once she'd remembered it and written it down, the pun "clicked" for

TAROT EXPERTS

There are many excellent tarot books on the market. Two of the best, however, are *The Tarot* by Cynthia Giles, and *Seventy-Eight Degrees of Wisdom* by Rachel Pollack.

The first book covers the history, mystery, and lore of the tarot. Giles touches on some unusual subjects in relation to the tarot, as in the chapter on the tarot and quantum physics. She also provides an excellent overview of the numerous decks that are available.

Pollack's book comes in two volumes. The first covers the Major Arcana and the second covers the Minor Arcana. These books offer an excellent overview of the meanings of the cards. If you're looking for a tarot book on spreads, the way the cards are laid out, *Power Tarot: 101 Spreads Plus* by Trish MacGregor and Phyllis Vega provides more than a hundred spreads to choose from.

The seminal work on the I Ching is the Richard Wilhelm edition called *The I Ching or The Book of Changes.* Wilhelm lived and studied in China for years and translated the text into English. His friend, the Swiss psychologist Carl Jung, wrote the introduction. It was here that Jung explained his theory of synchronicity, which he felt was at the heart of how the I Ching and other divination systems work.

The main problem with the Wilhelm edition lies in the metaphors used in the explanations of the hexagrams, which relate primarily to Chinese life. *A Guide to the I Ching,* by Carol K. Anthony, is much easier to use for dream interpretation and yet also comprehensive.

her. She knew what the dream was referring to.

At the end of this chapter is a section where you can jot down your personal symbols, thoughts, questions, or whatever comes to mind. You may want to keep this page and the charts handy when you're reading the last part of the book, which explores symbols in greater detail.

Divination and Dream Interpretation

Another method of helping you interpret dreams involves the use of a divination system, such as tarot cards or the I Ching. It may seem strange initially to use any divination system to interpret a dream. But divination systems are only tools that connect you to your intuitive self. They are all based on the same principle, that the cards or coins aren't separated from your consciousness, that they are, in fact, united through synchronicity. The layout of the cards or the toss of the coins is merely an act in linear time that allows you to perceive the pattern.

The I Ching is an ancient Chinese system of divination in which yarrow sticks or coins are tossed to create one or two of sixty-four hexagrams. Its language, like that of the tarot and like that of dreams, consists of patterns, of symbols.

With the tarot and other divination systems using cards, the archetypal symbols are clearly visible through the pictures on the cards. The patterns are revealed through the various layouts. Here's a tarot layout to try for dream interpretation.

Shuffle the deck and think about your question. Fan out the cards, select seven, and lay them out as depicted in Figure 5-1.

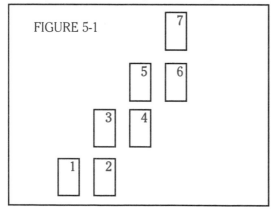

FIGURE 5-1

Positions one and two tell you what kind of dream this is—psychological, psychic, precognitive, guidance, transformative, or whatever. Positions three and four illuminate the core of the dream, its message. Positions five and six advise you on how to incorporate this message into your waking life. The card in the seventh position should remain face down until you're ready to turn it up. This is the synthesis card, the one that pulls together the others.

If you draw a court card—Page, Knight, King, or Queen—in any of the positions, pull another card to find out what role that person plays in the message. If you don't understand a card, select another for that particular position.

Association

Once you begin working with your dreams, you become more attuned to yourself and to your environment. Even if you can't recall your dreams at first or remember them in bits and pieces, you may find yourself flashing on an image during the day. Sometimes a conversation or some event or situation may trigger your recall.

When you start to recall symbols, try to associate them with something in your life. When you hit on something, associate that with something else, working your way back through your life until something "clicks." Freud first popularized this method.

Exercise 4: WHAT THEY SYMBOLIZE TO ME

Jot a word or phrase that defines this object next to the word. Don't refer to the glossary at the back of the book or any other dream dictionary. These are your personal interpretations. Don't give them much thought, just note the first thing that comes to mind. If you can't think of anything, move on to the next word on the list. Next, show the list to friends and family members and ask them to do the same.

Airplane	House
Airport	Knife
Altar	Lake
Balloon	Lamp
Basement	Letters
Beach	Mirror
Boat	Money
Book	Moon
Bridge	Ocean
Car	Plane
Chair	Sidewalk
Children	Street
Church	Sun
Class	Table
Computer	Telephone
Cross or Crucifix	Television
Door	Theater
Flowers	Train
Food	Tree
Grass	Water
Gun	Zoo
Hallway	

RIBBONS, TASSELS, EPAULETS

I f you should dream of ribbons floating from the costume of another person, you will have happy and pleasant friendships and everyday cares will not be troubling. To dream of buying ribbons denotes a happy life. Dreaming of decorating yourself with ribbons signifies you will soon have a good offer of marriage.

To dream of tassels means you will reach the top of your desires. But to dream of losing tassels means you might go through unpleasant experiences.

For a man to dream of epaulets means he might be in disfavor among his friends for a time. If a woman dreams of meeting a man wearing epaulets, beware, it denotes she is about to form an unwise alliance that might end in scandal.

Suppose the only thing you remember from a dream is that your significant other gave you a rose. What does a rose mean to you? Do you associate it with beauty? With thorns? With a sweet scent? Maybe you associate it with a garden. What does a garden mean to you? And so on, back through your memories until you hit something that feels right.

Amplification

This method, which Jung advocated, is similar to association, but with one important difference. Instead of working backward through your past, you look for associations in the present. With the symbol of the rose, for instance, you would list everything that a rose means to you *now*.

The tarot works well with this technique, especially if you use only the twenty-two major arcana cards, the archetypal images of the deck. Suppose for the rose symbol, you draw three major arcana cards: the Magician, the High Priestess, and the Empress. Without delving too deeply into the tarot, these cards would represent transformation, mystery, and motherhood/nurturing issues.

Once you hit on a symbol that resonates, you're on your way toward interpreting the dream.

Creating Your Own Dream Dictionary

For one person, children in a dream might represent love; for someone else, children might

Exercise 5: ANIMALS IN MY DREAMS

Jot a word or phrase next to each of the animals listed. Don't think about it, just write down whatever pops into you mind.

Alligator ....
Ant ....
Armadillo ....
Badger ....
Bat ....
Bear ....
Beaver ....
Bird ....
Butterfly ....
Cat ....
Coyote ....
Crow ....
Deer ....
Dog ....
Dolphin ....
Dragonfly ....
Duck ....
Eagle ....
Elk ....
Ferret ....
Fox ....
Frog ....
Giraffe ....
Gopher ....
Gorilla ....
Guinea pig ....
Hamster ....
Hawk ....
Heron ....
Horse ....

Hummingbird ....
Kitten ....
Lion ....
Lizard ....
Monkey ....
Moose ....
Mouse ....
Opossum ....
Otter ....
Owl ....
Peacock ....
Porcupine ....
Porpoise ....
Puppy ....
Rabbit ....
Raven ....
Seagull ....
Shark ....
Skunk ....
Snake ....
Spider ....
Squirrel ....
Swan ....
Turkey ....
Turtle ....
Unicorn ....
Whale ....
Wolf ....
Zebra ....

represent an annoyance. Unless you know what various objects mean to *you,* you won't have a clear idea about symbolic meanings in your dreams. To test this concept, go to Exercise 4, which contains a list of common objects. Once again, jot a word or phrase that defines this object next to the word. Don't refer to the glossary at the back of the book or any other dream dictionary. These are your personal interpretations. Don't give them much thought, just note the first thing that comes to mind. If you can't think of anything, move on to the next word on the list.

Next, show the list to friends and family members and ask them to do the same. You'll be surprised what different interpretations people have for symbols. For example, to one person the ocean may be symbolic of power, to another it might be a mother symbol, and yet another person might see the ocean as a symbol of fear or death. What's important for interpreting your dreams is how *you* see the symbols. There are no right or wrong answers.

Animals in Dreams

You can create additional entries in your personal dream dictionary by adding other common objects that appear in your dreams. You might also focus on specific types of symbols, for example, animals. To one person, a frog, for example, might represent luck; to another, the creature might represent transformation.

Rabbits played a key symbolic role for Edith, a French-Canadian massage therapist, who was feeling depressed when she had the following dream:

★ ★ ★

BLACK RABBITS

I'm in a school gymnasium, but there are no bleachers. It's a large, open room with lots of cages. I go over to the cages and see that they are filled with black rabbits. There are hundreds of them, but they are all dead.

I'm horrified at what I see. Then I notice an older man nearby. When I tell him that the rabbits are dead, he doesn't seem concerned. He says he can redo them for me. It won't be a problem. When I look again, I'm surprised to see that the cages are filled with black rabbits, more than before, and they're moving about and very much alive.

★ ★ ★

The events in Edith's life at the time of the dream are important in its interpretation. She had recently ended a bad relationship and was feeling depressed when she called her father one night. She told him that she felt dead inside, that no matter how hard she tried to keep a positive attitude, it wasn't working.

Her father, also a massage therapist, is known in Quebec for his healing touch. He

asked her if her third vertebra was sore and she said that it was. He told her that he would work on it in the astral plane while she slept, and that she would feel much better.

The next morning Edith didn't notice much change and although she felt somewhat better during the day, she went to bed again feeling empty and dead inside. Then she had the black rabbit dream. The following morning she felt much better and wondered why she had been feeling so burdened and depressed.

She interpreted the black rabbits as a symbol of magic and good luck. The fact that they were alive, for Edith, meant that the magic in her unconscious mind had been revived. She felt elated and called her father. He said he'd worked on her spine in the astral plane on the same night she'd had the rabbit dream.

When animals appear in dreams, they can be frightening, charming, or puzzling.

But, as in Edith's dream, they can also be revealing. Again, the meaning is related to your own thoughts about the particular creature in the dream.

The problem with a static outlook on interpreting dreams is that the meanings of the symbols change as you change. What makes a seven-year-old happy probably doesn't thrill a twenty-one-year old. Likewise, the joys or fears of a person at forty may be different from what pleases or concerns someone at seventy-five. So, periodically, update your personal dictionary—delete and add as necessary.

Dreams impart guidance even when you don't remember them. But once you have a fairly strong grasp of what certain symbols mean to you, you can become more than a passive observer in your dreams. You can request guidance from dreams—and receive answers!

CHAPTER SIX

The Dream Interview

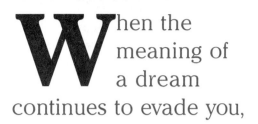

When the meaning of a dream continues to evade you, approach it as if you were being interviewed. This technique is often used by therapists to help the dreamer uncover the meaning of a particular dream or series of dreams. But you don't need a therapist to try the dream interview technique. A trusted friend or a spouse can act as the interviewer or you can act as your own interviewer.

> *I was not looking for my dreams to interpret my life, but rather for my life to interpret my dreams.*
>
> — SUSAN SONTAG,
> THE BENEFACTOR

The first step in this technique is to name your dream. This helps keep the dream straight in your journal and can also peg a major image or symbol. A valet parking attendant is the pivotal image in the following dream, thus its name.

★ ★ ★

VALET PARKING

It's night. I'm in front of a restaurant, wearing a uniform. A car pulls up, I open the doors, and the passengers get out. I realize I'm a valet parking attendant. I slide behind the steering wheel and drive the car out into the lot to park it.

The lot is large, crowded with vehicles. I have to park at the far end, where there are a few empty spots. It's a long walk back to the front of the restaurant, and I feel vaguely depressed that I'm doing this sort of work.

When I reach the front of the building, a wolf is trotting along beside me, a white wolf. The restaurant is gone and in its place is a library. I'm now wearing street clothes instead of the uniform. I go inside and the wolf accompanies me. No one objects to the wolf's presence.

I'm not sure why I've come to the library, I can't seem to remember. So I decide to check the new fiction shelf for something good to read. I find all of my books on the shelf, even the ones which are now out of print. I'm elated! I also find a book with my name on it that doesn't have a title, just a tremendous spiral on the front.

★ ★ ★

Ben was a 48-year-old suspense writer who was having money problems at the time of this dream. He was working on a novel that was quite different from his previous books. But since he was writing it on speculation, he needed other writing projects to pay

the bills until the novel sold. He'd taken on a ghostwriting project and a novelization, which paid well but took him away from his novel.

Once Ben had recorded the dream in his journal, he went through it and highlighted the most important items, that is, the setting, time of day, people, emotions, animals and major objects or symbols, and major actions. This technique is an expansion of one developed by dream therapist Gayle Delaney and her partner, Loma Flowers, directors of the Delaney and Flowers Center for the Study of Dreams. Ben listed the following:

1. *Settings:* outside restaurant, library, crowded parking lot

2. *Time:* night

3. *People:* me and other people whose faces are indistinct

4. *Emotions:* vague depression, elation

5. *Animals and major objects or symbols:* white wolf, cars, books, uniform and street clothes, spiral

6. *Major action:* parking cars, entering library, perusing new fiction shelf

Ben asked his wife to be the interviewer, so she worked from this list to devise questions. Delaney recommends that when doing this, pretend the interviewer is from another planet. This urges you, the dreamer, to give more detailed answers to the questions.

Ben used a tape recorder to record the interview. He said it would be easier to write everything down, but since he writes for a living, he wanted to try a different format in the hopes that more information would turn up.

Ben's Interview

Q What are your dominant feelings in this dream?

A Depression in the beginning, a kind of resignation to menial work as a valet parking lot attendant. I hate wearing the uniform. It smacks of regimentation.

Q Is there anything familiar about the feelings of depression in this dream?

A No.

Q What sort of feelings does the restaurant elicit for you?

A No feelings, really, just an awareness that it's associated with eating, food, that kind of thing. I think it represents sustenance.

Q How do you feel about the crowded parking lot?

A Irritated that I have to drive so far to find a parking space.

Q In general, what did the cars look like?

A I didn't notice. Nothing stood out about them. There were just a lot of them.

Q What do you think the parking lot represents?

A The publishing business as it exists now, vastly changed since the 1980s. It's becoming more and more difficult to get published—to find a parking space. These projects I've taken on are the equivalent of being a valet parking attendant.

In other words, I'm parking other people's cars—doing other people's projects— and that's why none of the cars stood out in any way. The restaurant symbolizes paying bills and putting food on the table as a result of these other projects.

Q How do you feel about the white wolf?

A Delighted, surprised to see it trotting along beside me. I've always had an affinity with wolves. In a sense, they're my guardian spirits.

Q It's interesting that the white wolf appears at your side on your way back to the restaurant, which has turned into a library. What do you think that means?

A The appearance of the wolf seems to be a signal that things in the dream land-scape are about to change—and then they do. The restaurant is suddenly a library. Maybe it means things in my waking life are about to change, too.

Q What do libraries represent to you?

A Books. Knowledge. Pleasure. In my waking life, the new fiction shelf is usu-

ally my first stop at the library. I didn't expect to see all my books there, even the ones that have gone out of print.

Q What do you think that means?

A Maybe that some of my older books will be in print again. I was elated to find all the books on that shelf.

Q What do you feel about the spiral symbol on the untitled book?

A I think it represents the novel I've been working on between other projects. One of the titles I've been considering is *Spiral*.

Once you become proficient at dream interpretation, the interview technique prob-ably will be second nature. You won't have to write out the entire interview or record it, although you may still want to do that with complex dreams.

Veronica Tonay, a psychotherapist and lecturer at the University of California at Santa Cruz, recommends against putting too much stock in any one dream. "Usually a series of dreams is more reliable for picking out themes," said Tonay.

"You want to look for what is common in the dreams, such as something always blocking your way or threatening your chance to succeed. Then you should uncover how you are coping with this threat. What can you learn from what you are doing or not doing in the dream?"

LACE, SILK, VELVET

L ace, silk, velvet—to dream of these things overall denotes good times ahead.

For a man to dream of his lover wearing lace means two good things will happen. He will have her faithfulness in love, and he will probably get a job promotion. You can't ask for much more.

For a woman to dream of wearing lace denotes happiness. She supposedly will reach her ambitions and her lover will fulfill her every wish. Dreaming of lace does denote good things happening! If you dream of buying lace, you will have wealth. If you dream of making lace, you will meet a good-looking and wealthy man who will propose. If you dream you are selling lace, watch out, your ambitions will outrun your resources.

If you dream of wearing silk clothes, your high ambitions will be met. If you dream of old silk, it means you are feeling pride in your ancestors and also you will soon be courted by a wealthy, but elderly person.

If you dream of wearing velvet, this too denotes good things will happen. You will be very successful in all your enterprises and possibly high honor will be conferred on you.

Children's Dreams and Interviewing

Children's dreams often hold clues to the same anxieties and insecurities that plague their parents. Some kids will talk spontaneously about their dreams; other kids may have to be prodded. But one fact holds true for all kids. If they live in households where dream sharing is simply part of the family routine, they'll be more apt to remember and relate their dreams.

Can you figure out what the next dream was telling the dreamer and her mother?

★　★　★

ALLIGATOR

Mommy and I are on a beach. It's hot. The sand burns my feet. The ocean is calm, real pretty. Mommy and I are going to go swimming. But I look back and see an alligator chasing us. It's coming so fast and I'm scared, I'm screaming, I don't want to be eaten up.

We run and run, but the alligator comes faster and faster. Then the lifeguard kills it.

★　★　★

The dreamer was Jenny, a seven-year-old girl who lived in Florida. Her mother, Helen, had been divorced for a year or so from Jenny's father, who was considerably older. Jenny spent most weekends with her Dad, and he and her mother were on amicable terms. She appeared to have adjusted to the divorce.

Since Helen encourages her to share her dreams, *Alligator* was casually related over breakfast one morning. Helen's initial reaction was that it was a positive dream, but she wanted to explore it to be sure. Although she'd never heard of an interview technique with dreams, that's basically what she carried out right then, as she usually does with her daughter's dreams.

The spontaneity of such an exchange is probably more important than the dream itself. Through it, Jenny learns that her dreams are a very personal source of information. This alone is empowering. She also learns that it's natural to talk about them, to share them, and to pay attention to them.

Within seconds, Helen intuitively identified the metaphors and symbols in the dream:

1. *Ocean:* represents Jenny's emotions. The fact that the ocean is calm indicates there aren't any upheavals inside Jenny right now.

2. *Beach:* represents the shore of their new world. Jenny feels comfortable in this new world until she looks back and sees the alligator. The act of looking back may indicate that in the past, she felt threatened by the move and the separation and divorce.

3. *Alligator:* the threat. It chases Jenny and Helen along the "shore of their new

life." But it doesn't catch them, doesn't eat them up.

4. *Lifeguard:* he "guards life" by killing the threat. Jenny doesn't confront the alligator herself, but an adult male does it for her. Helen felt this indicated Jenny's sense of security about the role her father now plays in her life. She also realized she needed to nurture Jenny's self-reliance, so that she didn't always depend on an adult to fix things for her.

Dream Sharing

To share dreams with your child or children not only helps you spot potential trouble areas but also creates a special dimension to your relationship. One four-year-old, an only child named Megan, had a series of nightmares in which she was being chased by huge tigers, ugly monkeys, and aliens. For several weeks, she woke up crying every night and crawled into her parents' bed because she was afraid to stay alone in her room.

Her parents told her the usual things—the creatures and the aliens weren't real, they couldn't hurt her, it was just a dream. But to Megan, the dreams *were* real.

During this time, Megan's parents were doing some redecorating around the house and put up a strip of wallpaper in Megan's room with unicorns on it. She loved the unicorns, asked questions about them, wanted to go to the zoo to see one. Her parents suddenly realized they'd found the answer to

ending the nightmares. They suggested that the next time she had a bad dream, she should call on a unicorn that would protect her from whatever was chasing her.

One morning at breakfast, she proudly announced that the night before she'd seen a unicorn in her nightmare. She'd called to it and the unicorn had galloped over. She'd climbed onto its back and it had flown her away. Now Megan is seven and has learned to create a variety of guardian creatures in nightmares. She is aware that her dream life is important, even if she doesn't yet know why.

Among the Senoi, a primitive tribe in the mountainous jungles of Malaysia, dream sharing is the pivot around which the rest of

HOW TO CONDUCT A DREAM INTERVIEW

1. As the interviewer, you must know what your subject, the dreamer, wants to know about the dream.

   Have the dreamer write out the dream, so that you have it in front of you during the interview.

   Before you begin the interview, underline the words or images that strike you. Ask the dreamer to do the same. Use these words as triggers during your interview.

   Record the interview.

2. Use your intuition during the interview.

   If the dreamer goes off on a tangent, follow it. Don't try to push the dreamer back into the parameters you have set. This is *her* dream; follow the tangent, see where it leads.

   If the dreamer suddenly stops or seems uncomfortable with what he or she is saying, gently probe for what the person is feeling. Strong emotions are often clues to the real heart of the dream.

   Keep in mind that you are both explorers. Maintain your curiosity, your excitement, your sense of adventure. And by all means, keep the mood playful.

3. Encourage the dreamer to eventually conduct his or her own interviews. This is a playful technique in which the dreamer alternately plays both roles. Sometimes, this is best done by writing out the interview.

   If you use the writing method, compose your questions beforehand. If you go off on tangents, follow them.

   If you feel a strong emotion while writing your answers, then pause and explore the emotion. Are you angry? Fearful? Exuberant? Why?

4. Remember that whatever you feel about one of your dreams is important because it's *your* emotion about *your* dream, an intimate peek at your unconscious self.

---

life revolves. According to researchers, each day begins with the members of the family, including children, sharing their dreams from the night before. Family members are asked about how they behaved in their dreams, and suggestions are given for correcting behavior and attitude in future dreams. Then the group suggests actions based on the events in the dreams. Once the family dream sharing is finished, the village council meets and the serious dream stuff begins. With each dream that's reported and

discussed, the tribe's picture of itself expands and clarifies. Symbols are analyzed, each council member gives his opinion. People in the tribe who agree on the meaning of a particular dream adopt it as a group project.

"The Senoi people determine most activities of daily life from the interpretations and decisions that arise out of their council discussions," writes Patricia Garfield in *Creative Dreaming*.

In his conference workshops, Brugh Joy, author of *Joy's Way*, encourages dream sharing. But since this sort of thing typically isn't practiced in Western culture, it can be a disconcerting experience for some people. Orloff, who attended one of Joy's conferences and writes about it in *Second Sight*, initially felt intimidated about it. Here she was, sitting around with a bunch of strangers, and Joy chose her to be the first person in the group to share a dream from the previous night.

Orloff couldn't remember any dreams from the night before, so she related a recent dream that had puzzled her. Joy proceeded to interpret the dream and by the end of it, Orloff felt as if she'd been stripped naked. She was mortified. By the next morning, she was so angry she considered leaving the conference.

She realized, though, that her anger meant Joy had touched a nerve and she took a much closer look at everything he'd said.

Her experience is cautionary. It's far more comfortable to share dreams with people you know and trust. On the other hand, a knowledgeable outsider, such as Brugh Joy, may offer a concise interpretation that you, or those close to you, might not suggest.

The Senoi don't criticize or condemn an action in a dream; they suggest alternative behaviors and actions. Any negative aspect is to be transformed into something positive. Fear is transmuted into courage, danger is avoided, and pleasure and a positive outcome are achieved. These dream actions are then carried out, in one form or another, in waking life.

If, for instance, one person dreams that he's hostile toward another member of the tribe, then in his waking life he goes out of his way to be amicable. Imagine if warring countries were able to do this!

Information about the Senoi culture was first gathered by a British anthropologist, Herbert Noone, in 1939, for his doctoral dissertation at Cambridge. He, with Dennis Holman, wrote *In Search of the Dream People*, which was published in 1972. In the years since, certain researchers have claimed that the Senoi culture described by Noone and Holman never existed as they depicted it. The issue is still being debated. But as Jill Morris notes in *The Dream Workbook:* ". . . There is no dispute over the effectiveness of the techniques themselves . . ."

The dreamer of the next dream was a self-employed businessman in his late forties, who windsurfed in his spare time. At the time of the dream, Rick had been recording his nightly sojourns sporadically over a number of years.

* * *

RIDING THE WAVE
I'm standing on shore, beneath a purple sky, watching huge ocean waves rolling in and crashing on the beach. Suddenly, the ocean rises and flows into the streets and I'm surfing on top of a tremendous wave. I feel exhilarated by the experience. Then the wave lowers me gently to the street.

When I glance around, I find myself in a winding corridor, which gets progressively narrower. I turn around and head the other way. A woman is moving in my direction and I ask her if she knows where I can find University Avenue. She says she doesn't know, but suggests I send a telegraph.

> *The myth is the public dream and the dream is the private myth.*
>
> — JOSEPH CAMPBELL, THE POWER OF MYTH

When Rick woke up, the word *telegraph* stuck in his mind and allowed him to recall the dream in detail. When striking messages of images occur in dreams, they often do so to grab your attention. If the woman had just told Rick to ask someone else, he might not have placed any significance on the comment.

Instead, he puzzled over the meaning of the dream. Riding the waves gave him a sense of being on top of things, of going with the flow, enjoying it. But what about the corridor and why did he want to find University Avenue?

He realized that the corridor symbolized the unconscious and he was there seeking knowledge, symbolized by University Avenue. When the woman told him to send a telegraph, she was telling him that he could ask his dreaming self for an answer to any of his questions. Thus, the dream was offering guidance, and the guidance was to ask for a dream.

We're constantly guided by our dreams, whether we remember them or not. But once you begin to recall dreams with ease, it's possible to request dreams that will guide you and even give you hints of future events on particular issues or dilemmas. It might be a relationship issue, a health matter, a career question, or something else. Or you may simply request a dream that you will remember. The act of asking for a

GLOVES

F ew people wear gloves today, unless its 10 degrees outside. But we do still dream of wearing gloves, even in summer. If you dream you are wearing gloves, regardless of the weather, it denotes caution to be exercised in your financial dealings.

To dream of old, ragged gloves signifies you might possibly suffer a loss and worse, be betrayed. But to dream of finding a pair of gloves can mean a marriage is to happen or that you will start a new love affair. This is good news if you are single; it can however complicate your life if you are married.

dream, for whatever purpose, is called dream incubation.

This process was popular in many ancient cultures including Mesopotamia, ancient Egypt, Rome, and Greece. People often traveled to temples dedicated to specific gods, where they spent the night in hopes of receiving a dream that would heal, illuminate, guide, and provide solutions.

In some temples, priests were available to help seekers interpret their dreams. There were even professional dream seekers, who were hired by people too ill or otherwise unable to travel to the dream temples. Those who participated usually were required to undergo fasts, baths, or other rituals.

Today, there may be no recognized dream temples for seekers, but anyone can practice dream incubation in their own home. The first step in dream incubation is knowing what to ask for. Are you concerned about a health problem? A career move? Your family?

The Method

After considering what you've written, pick one of the areas and select a concern. Now you are ready to begin practicing dream incubation.

Some experts recommend writing your request for a dream on a slip of paper and placing it on your nightstand or under your pillow. The idea is that by making it a ritual, you are formalizing it. But most of the time, a sincere need and intent will suffice. And,

of course, you have to remember the dream. But even the need to remember the dream can be included in your request.

Gayle Delaney, in her book *Breakthrough Dreaming,* suggests that you jot down five or ten lines about your request in your dream journal. Then condense this to a phrase or question that states what you want to know. Fall asleep repeating this phrase or question to yourself.

Even if you don't remember anything the first time you try this, keep at it. With persistence, you'll recall a dream that addresses your concern. Some of your answers, however, may not be what you bargained for.

In the next example, the dreamer, a published novelist, asked about her future with the company that was publishing her books. She had published a number of successful paperback novels with the publishing house, but her editor had died the year before and she felt her books weren't being promoted as aggressively as they had been in the past.

★ ★ ★

DINNER

I'm having dinner with the editor in chief of a publishing house, and several other corporate people from that company. My editor, who worked for the house, is also there, even though he had been dead about a year at the time of the dream. I don't seem surprised to see him, though. Even though everyone is pleasant, I feel uncomfortable, like I'm not fully aware of everything that's happening under the surface.

We're eating on an outside terrace suspended high above a city. It's night, I can see the lights below. A wind is blowing and the terrace begins to tremble, then shake. Someone at the table laughs nervously and jokes that an earthquake is in progress. Someone else replies that it can't be an earthquake, we're not in California.

My books, paperback originals, are stacked in the center of the table and they slide around as the terrace trembles. No one but me seems to notice. Or maybe the others don't care that the books are sliding all over the place. At any rate, I'm the only one who reaches out to straighten them.

Just then, a waiter hurries over with a tray. There are only two things on it—a hardback book and an envelope, which he hands me. I open it. Inside is a card, like an invitation, with one word on it:
Hyperborean.

★   ★   ★

The novelist interpreted the shaking terrace in the dream to mean that she was on "shaky ground" with her current publisher and had been since her editor's death. The peculiar word on the invitation was actually similar to the name of another publisher and seemed to be an indirect response to her question.

Several weeks later, she mentioned the dream to a friend, an editor at another house. He told her that the day before, the head of her publishing house had been fired and rumor had it that more resignations were on the way. The "shaking terrace" apparently applied to more than just the author's standing with the publisher. Four months after this dream, the author signed a contract with Hyperion Books. Not only is the name close to Hyperborean, but both names relate to Greek myths. So this dream not only offered guidance, but provided a peek at the future, as well.

Another type of dream incubation involved a cat. Marie, a grade school teacher, had a Himalayan cat named Demian that was blind in one eye. She'd bought him from an animal shelter when she was in graduate school. When Demian was fifteen years old, he developed urinary problems that led to a complete collapse of his kidneys. The vet told her the only option was dialysis, a painful, expensive procedure that he didn't recommend.

She brought him into the vet's office to be put to sleep and stayed with him while the vet administered the shot. At the moment that he died, she says she felt his spirit leave his body. She took him home and buried him in the yard.

During the next few months, she sometimes felt him around the house—a softness against the backs of her legs, as though he were brushing up against her. One night she requested a dream about Demian. She wanted to know how he was and if something of his essence or soul had survived, and if it would be okay for

BRIDE, ELOPEMENT, MARRIAGE LICENSE

It's good news if you dream of a bride—whether you are the bride or it's your uncle's step-cousin's daughter. To dream of a bride denotes you will soon come into a big inheritance. If in your dream a man kisses the bride, that denotes a happy reconciliation between family and friends.

But these dreams of brides have to take place at weddings; to dream of an elopement denotes unfavorable events occurring in your life. In fact you might lose your good reputation. And if you dream of your partner eloping with someone else, possibly you will soon learn of your partner being unfaithful.

If you should dream of such practical wedding matters such as a marriage license, this too doesn't denote easy times ahead. You might make an unhappy alliance and find your pride humiliated.

So only dream of brides at public weddings and don't even worry about the marriage license.

Exercise 6: DREAM INCUBATION

The brainstorming exercise is intended to help you identify areas of your life that you would like to change. Once you recognize them, you'll have a better idea about what to request from your dreaming self.

1. Relationships
- ☆ My most intimate relationships are generally
- ☆ I don't understand why my spouse or significant other
- ☆ I feel good about my relationship with
  because
- ☆ I would like to change my relationship with
  because
- ☆ I would like to end my relationship with
  because
- ☆ The pattern in my intimate relationships is
- ☆ My relationship with my parents is
  because
- ☆ My relationship with my brothers or sisters is
  because
- ☆ If possible, I would change
- ☆ I am happiest in relationships that
- ☆ In a perfect world, my relationships would

2. Work/career
- ☆ I .... my job.
- ☆ With my work/job/career, I would like to change
- ☆ My ideal job/career is
- ☆ I would like to be earning
- ☆ I .... my boss.
- ☆ I don't get along with
- ☆ In terms of work/career, my bliss would be

3. Health/physical self
I like ..../don't like .... the way I look/feel.

☆ If I could change anything about the way I look, it would be.................................

☆ My health is ....

☆ I have a chronic problem with ....

☆ I have been to..................................doctors in the last six months.

☆ I have missed..................................days of work in the last six months.

☆ My ideal physical self would be...

4. Spiritual life

☆ I believe in...

☆ I feel ....about my spiritual life.

☆ In my spiritual life, I would like to develop ....

☆ I would like to change ....

☆ I would like to experience ....

5. Life in general

☆ In six months I would like to be ....

☆ In a year, I would like to be..

☆ Within five years, I envision myself...

6. I need guidance on:

a) ....

b) ....

c) ....

d) ....

e) ....

her to get another cat. She had the following dream:

* * *

DEMIAN THE CAT

I wake up in the middle of the night and go downstairs for a glass of water. When I enter the kitchen, Demian is eating out of his bowl. I leap back, startled to see him. "You're dead," I whisper.

He looks up at me with his spooky eyes, one an eerie blue, the other a milky white. "I'm not dead," he replies. "I'm just fine."

Then he rubs up against my leg, purring, and I wake up.

* * *

Marie felt uplifted by the dream and two days later, on her fortieth birthday, she went out and bought a tabby kitten.

In both of these examples, the issues were fairly simple. The dreamers sincerely wanted answers and believed their dreams could provide them. Belief, however, isn't always a prerequisite to dream incubation. During periods when you're intensely focused on resolving a problem or dilemma or you're going through a turbulent time, you may have dreams that address the issues you're concerned about.

In a South Florida writers' group, several writers reported that when they were really "plugged in" to a novel, they often dreamed about the scenes they were going to write the next day. "I usually find myself in a library, where my book is on a shelf—fin-ished, published, and distributed," said one woman. "I open it up and page through it until I find where I left off that day, then read the next fifteen or twenty pages. I never remember what the pages say when I wake up, but whenever this happens, the words just flow out of me the next day."

A science fiction writer in the same group said that whenever he gets blocked, he takes a nap. Even though he usually doesn't request a dream that will help him break through his block, that's invariably what happens because he's been so focused on it. "Quite a few times, I dream that I'm working on the book, literally typing away on the computer. Then when I wake up, whole chunks of the story have fallen into place."

Some creative dreaming was a hallmark of the works of Robert Louis Stevenson. He considered his work a collaboration between his dreams and waking state, and claimed that he could dream scenes in sequence, picking up a story where it left off the night before. *The Strange Case of Dr. Jekyll and Mr. Hyde* came to Stevenson in a dream when he was in need of a story. In his waking life, he had been toying with the idea of man as a double being. Then, the actual story came to him in a dream in which he saw Hyde ingesting a powder and undergoing a metamorphosis in the presence of his pursuers.

But you don't have to be a writer to incubate dreams. According to Patricia Garfield in her book *Creative Dreaming,* it is not an uncommon occurrence. "Ordinary dreamers are able to train themselves to have creative dreams in the area of their work," she says.

CHAPTER EIGHT

Healing
Dreams

Imagine a world where if you got sick you could seek out the help of a healer/physician who would work with you in attempting to understand the source of your dis-ease. The healer would intuitively probe your beliefs about yourself and your world and would help you identify general and specific patterns in your unconscious.

Herbs, body work, special foods, and visualization techniques might be recommended. The healer might also recommend intense dream work to galvanize the body's defenses. He or she could urge you to request healing dreams that would alleviate or cure your physical problem.

Judith Orloff relates such a healing dream that a friend of hers had. The woman had a lipoma, a fatty tumor, at the base of her spine. It was causing her considerable pain, but she was reluctant to undergo surgery. She dreamed that she inserted a three-foot syringe into her neck and worked it down her spine to the lipoma. Then she drained the lipoma. When she woke, she remembered the dream and immediately checked for the lipoma, feeling around her lower back. She couldn't find it.

> *I have found that dreams can provide adequate warning of an illness giving the patient and doctor some direction before it becomes too advanced.*
>
> — DR. WILLIAM A. MCGAREY,
> *IN SEARCH OF HEALING*

Shortly afterward, her doctor confirmed the lipoma was gone.

The woman's recollection of the dream strengthened her belief in the power of dreams to heal. But you don't have to remember a healing dream to benefit from the effects. As Brugh Joy, author of *Joy's Way,* writes: "If we recognize that we are much more than we understand at the outer levels of consciousness, then we can see that the forces experienced in dreams may reflect healing and balancing processes that never reach the outer levels of our awareness, yet are profoundly important to the overall Beingness."

This statement is similar to something Seth said in *The Unknown Reality:* "Cellular life is affected by your dreams. Healing can take place in the dream state, where events at another order of existence alter the cells themselves."

Dr. William A. McGarey, director of the Association for Research and Enlightenment in Phoenix, points out an example of a woman who reported that she had the same dream on two successive nights in which she blurted out, "I have MS." McGarey checked and found early symptoms of multiple sclerosis. "We took measures to stop it from developing," he says. "She is presently doing quite well."

The dreamer in the next example was Toni, a woman who had requested a guidance dream about her parents' health problems. Toni had recently developed a humming in her left ear, but wasn't thinking about that when she requested the dream on her parents.

★ ★ ★

EAR SURGERY

I'm with a friend who is studying alternative health and I'm telling her about the annoying humming in my ear. She asks if I've ever heard of . . . and then said a word I couldn't remember when I woke. I reply that I've never heard of this therapy, so she shows me how it works.

She takes a long object that resembles a stick of incense and inserts it into my left ear. Then she rolls it gently between her fingers and the stick slips in deeper and deeper. I hear a popping sound, then a liquid seeps out, a milky liquid.

When I wake, the humming in my ear is gone.

★ ★ ★

Toni felt the dream's message was twofold: It confirmed her belief that healing dreams were possible, and it indicated that her parents might be helped through alternative therapies that, on the surface, look absurd.

It's interesting to note that the humming in her ear returned a day after the dream, but to a lesser degree. She feels its cause has to do with equalizing pressure between the inner and outer ear, similar to what happens to a passenger's eardrums when taking off or landing during an airplane trip. But the root of the problem, she says, has to do with her need to find balance in her life, to "equalize" the various demands on her time.

Healing Symbols

Hippocrates, the ancient Greek physician, believed that the body sensed the incipience of disease and often warned the dreamer about it. The appearance in a dream of the sun, moon, or stars symbolized the dreamer's organic state, he said.

If the dream stars glow brightly, it means the body is functioning as it should. But if the stars seem dim or cloudy or if some cosmic disaster occurs, it indicates that disease is forming somewhere in the body. Hippocrates theorized that if such symbols portend disease, then other symbols can be used therapeutically for healing.

Dr. Carl Simonton pioneered a program in which he combines visualization and relaxation techniques in the treatment of cancer patients. His first attempt was with a sixty-one-year-old man who had throat cancer and for whom conventional therapies had failed. The man had been given about a ten-percent chance of survival.

COFFEE & COFFEEHOUSE

Whether it's Starbucks or Dunkin' Donuts, if you dream of drinking coffee, it denotes that your friends disapprove of your marriage intentions. That's assuming you have marriage intentions. If you are already married and you dream of drinking coffee, be prepared for many disagreements and quarrels. If you dream you are roasting coffee—does anyone know how to roast coffee?—you soon will marry a stranger. To dream of ground coffee signifies you will be successful in overcoming some adversity.

To dream of visiting a coffeehouse denotes that women are conspiring against you and your possessions. This is true if a man or woman dreams of visiting a coffeehouse.

Exercise 7: DREAMING OF GOOD HEALTH

Here are some general symbols that are indicative of good health. Use these to brainstorm and come up with more symbols of your own. You may want to create a section in your dream journal where you can list symbols of good health that arise from your dreams.

If you're an avid swimmer, for instance, you may find that the various moods and color of the ocean or a swimming pool depict states of your health. If you enjoy gardening, the state of your dream garden may tell you a great deal about your health. If you love horses, then a dream image of a robust, exuberant horse may represent a healthy image of your body. Be innovative, let your imagination run wild.

GENERAL SYMBOLS OF GOOD HEALTH	MY SYMBOLS OF GOOD HEALTH
Sun	
Clear, cool water	
A flourishing garden	
Brilliant stars	
The color gold	
The color green	
The color pink	
A God image	
An angel	
A healer	

Simonton's treatment consisted of mental exercises repeated three times a day for seven weeks. First, the patient was to spend several minutes silently repeating the word *relax*, while relaxing the muscles in his throat, jaw, and around his eyes. Next, he was told to visualize something pleasurable for a minute and a half. Then he was to replace that image with a mental picture of how he imagined his tumor looked.

Once he was able to hold a vivid mental picture of the tumor, he was supposed to imagine particles of radiation bombarding it. The last step was to visualize white blood cells clearing away the cells killed by the radiation. At the end of the seven weeks, the tumor's growth had been arrested and the patient was released.

But don't wait until you're sick to reinforce your health. As Patricia Garfield notes in *Creative Dreaming*, "You can suggest to yourself dream images believed to be reflective of good health and thereby encourage well-being in yourself."

Dream Incubation for Health

The first step in using your dreams for healing is to accept that it's possible to induce a dream—any dream.

Before actually attempting to induce a healing dream, find a quiet spot where you won't be interrupted. A shady spot in your yard might do, a secluded place on a beach, or your own bedroom.

As you settle down, begin by relaxing your body. An effective relaxation technique is to consciously relax muscles from your head to your toes and feel the tension drain out through the soles of your feet. Or you can simply focus on the warmth of the sunlight or the scent of the air.

Once you're fully relaxed, you're ready for the next step. Have a clear idea of the dream you want to induce and concentrate on it. The concentration may be enhanced by the repetition of a word or phrase that has something to do with the dream you're trying to induce. If you choose a phrase, be careful of how you word it. Keep it positive. Instead of saying that you're tumor is gone, for example, it would be better to say: "I am healed." Use the positive healing symbols you've noted in the symbols exercise.

Garfield points out another way to induce a dream, and that's to "visualize the desired dream as though it is happening." This is no different, really, than a visualization in a fully conscious state of something you want to happen. The same principles apply. Belief is paramount—belief that it will happen, that it's possible, that your mind, your being, is wise and capable.

Believe, intend, imagine, and charge the visualization with emotions. Also, keep the visualization *in the present* rather than in some dim future. As Seth says in *The Nature of Personal Reality*, "You can cure yourself of

an 'incurable' disease if you realize that your point of power is in the present."

If you're bothered that this advice comes from "an energy personality no longer focused in physical existence," as Seth describes himself, then listen to the philosopher William James. He believed that the unconscious manifests any image held in the mind and backed by faith. Or take Judith Orloff's advice: "Allow yourself to believe . . . attend to your dreams . . . When you dream, you merge with a benevolent intelligence that touches you and in some special circumstances it even heals."

If the healing dream doesn't come to you the first time you try it, keep at it. Share the process with someone you trust—a spouse, sibling, parent, friend, son, or daughter. By sharing, you make it even more real. Read about dreams and other people's experiences with healing.

When Louise Hay, author of *You Can Heal Your Life,* was diagnosed with cancer, her physician wanted to perform a hysterectomy as soon as possible. But Hay resisted. She told him she wanted some time to work on the problem herself.

She completely revamped the externals in her life—nutrition, exercise, and work schedule. Then she began to work with her beliefs through visualization, affirmations, and prayer. She created mental stages on which she spoke to the various people in her past who had hurt her deeply and she saw herself forgiving them. She also experienced self-forgiveness by learning to love herself.

Within six months, her cancer was in remission.

One of Hay's most valuable contributions to literature on alternative healing is a list of physical ailments and diseases. This list includes the probable emotional cause, as well as an affirmation to help reverse the emotional pattern. You may not agree with everything she says, but those who begin working with the material soon realize this is powerful stuff.

Your dreams reflect what's going on in your body; your body reflects the texture of your dreams. The inner is a reflection of the outer.

Dream Therapists

If you're trying to heal yourself of a serious ailment, you might consider working with a qualified dream therapist. When one of Orloff's patients tried to commit suicide, she was forced to re-evaluate the way she practiced psychiatry. She knew she needed to integrate her psychic abilities into her medical practice, but didn't know how to do it or where to start.

Perhaps because her need was so great and she was open to synchronicities, she found what she needed: A friend told her about Brugh Joy's two-week retreat.

"Working with Brugh," she writes, "I . . . got a firsthand demonstration of how the psychic and the medical could be blended in a positive way."

Exercise 8: MY HEALING DREAM

Make notes on your first attempt to induce a healing dream. How did your body feel? What symbols did you use? Which symbols worked? If you were successful in inducing a dream, how close was it to what you desired? What was the content of the dream? What people were in it? What objects? Were there any animals? Brainstorm on the exercise, then include the dream and your remarks in your journal.

Once your physical condition begins to improve, track your progress. It's the best confirmation you'll get that your body has the capacity to heal itself.

Relaxation: ....

....

....

Induction: ....

....

....

Symbols I used: ....

....

Symbols in the dream: ....

....

The dream: ....

....

....

How I felt when I woke: ....

....

....

Elements I will change: ....

....

Other remarks: ....

....

....

....

Orloff's patient was a young woman who had been diagnosed with leukemia three years earlier. Her chemotherapy wasn't working and the last hope that conventional medicine could offer her was a bone marrow transplant. She began Joy's dream therapy with an exhaustive interview that covered her medical history and proceeded through her psychological makeup. "Guided by intuition, he uncovered areas in Debbie that might have taken years to emerge in traditional psychotherapy," Orloff writes.

Halfway through the interview, Joy suddenly asked Debbie if she'd ever lost a child. The young woman paled and admitted that twenty years before, she'd had a stillbirth. The experience was so painful she'd blocked it out. "Brugh saw in this the essence of a mind-body link, that there was a strong emotional component to Debbie's illness. Over the next hour, I watched him deftly uncover a lifelong pattern of losses for which she had never grieved . . ."

The therapist's value lies in the objective insight provided. But if you prefer to work on your own or with a spouse or trusted friend, then the interview technique in chapter 6 will provide an objective base.

When you recall a healing dream, especially one that has come to you without induction, you and your interviewer should pay special attention to it. It's the voice of your inner, wiser self crying out to be heard.

It's possible to act as your own interviewer. Gayle Delaney suggests that you list particular questions about a dream; for example, what is the location of the dream and your feelings about it? Are there colors in the dream, and if so, what do they mean to you? Are there common objects used for unusual purposes, and if so, what are they? Then jot each question on a cue card. Later, you can use the cards as an interviewer might, probing the meaning of the dream.

Read through the *Ear Surgery* dream again. Then, acting as though you are the interviewer, create a list of questions in your journal. Compare these questions with those in the interview with Toni in the next section.

Toni's Interview

(Her husband acted as the interviewer.)

Q One of the things missing from this dream is a specific location. Do you recall where the dream took place?

A Now that you've brought it up, yes, I think I remember a room. We were in a room with pale pink walls. There was comfortable furniture around, but I was lying on a massage table, my head elevated slightly on a pillow. I don't remember anything else about the room.

Q Was there a window?

A I don't remember one. It's as if I was supposed to focus only on the procedure.

Q You described the object your friend used as resembling a stick of incense. Can you describe it in more detail?

A It was twelve to eighteen inches long. The end that my friend rolled between her fingers was thinner than a pencil, but it gradually thickened, just like a stick of incense does.

Q Do you know what color it was?

A A rich, dark brown, like chocolate.

Q What does the word *incense* mean to you?

A It means . . . oh, good point. I see what you're getting at. I completely overlooked that in my interpretation. What am I incensed about, right? What is it that has made me so angry I don't want to hear about it?

Q Exactly. It's definitely a metaphor, a play on words.

A I don't know what I'm angry about. Maybe it's just things with my parents in general. It infuriates me that two people who have taken such good care of themselves have ended up in a health crisis. I don't understand everything that's behind it.

Q What significance, if any, do you think there is about this humming occurring in your left ear?

A I'm 90 percent deaf in that ear. The humming has made me think a lot about the accident that caused the deafness. It was from a fractured skull, when I was five and it is supposedly irreversible. But lately I've been wondering if it can be healed.

Q When your friend began inserting the stick in your ear, how did you feel about it?

A Very uneasy. I nearly told her to forget it. But I sensed she knew what she was doing. It struck me later that my unconscious created the ideal figure to act as the healer. If a typical physician in a white lab coat had attempted the procedure, I would have walked out. But I trusted her and associate her with the healing arts and alternative medicine.

Q You describe a milky liquid that comes out of your ear. Was there any kind of noise associated with this? Anything that indicated a blockage had been punctured?

A A soft popping sound. It got my attention.

Q Was there any pain?

A None. Absolutely none.

Q The liquid was white, like milk. What do you associate with that color?

A Understanding. It's the amalgam of all the other colors in the spectrum.

Q Do you have any idea what time of night you had this dream?

A Morning. I woke at seven, realized I didn't have to get up, then remembered I hadn't gotten the dream I'd requested and felt disappointed. Then I went back to sleep and had the dream.

As a result of the interview, Toni remembered more details of the dream. Thus, her insight deepened. And that, really, is the ultimate goal of all dream work.

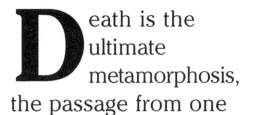

Death is the ultimate metamorphosis, the passage from one state of being to another. In the tarot, the Death card means transformation, a major change that hurls you from one way of life to another. In a dream, death is usually a symbol for the same thing.

Death Dreams

"Ninety-nine percent of the time, dreams about death are simply metaphors for major changes happening in your relationships, work, or personality," writes Stase Michaels in *The Bedside Book of Dreams.* When you have such a dream, you need to consider whether an area of your life is undergoing transformation. Are you in the middle of a divorce? About to have a baby? Are you about to get married? Are you considering a career change?

Quite often, dreams about death involve other symbols, like a car, which is a perfect dream metaphor for where you're going in life and how the journey is unfolding. For a

For in that sleep of death what dreams may come.

—WILLIAM SHAKESPEARE

sixteen-year-old girl, a death dream in which a car figured prominently underscored the recent move her family made from the state where she'd been born and raised. For a forty-eight-year-old accountant, a death dream symbolized a major job transition from a large firm to self-employment.

In the next dream, the death symbolism pointed to a young man's changing feelings about his girlfriend:

★   ★   ★

CARNIVAL
Jan and I are at the carnival that's rolled into town. It was her idea to go and she's like a kid, eating cotton candy, running from ride to ride, insistent that I go with her. I don't like carnivals and wish we could leave.

She wants to go on the roller coaster, I don't. We argue out there in front of everyone and I'm totally embarrassed. Just to keep her quiet, I relent and go on the roller coaster with her.

I hate the roller coaster, everyone screaming, Jan clutching my arm and shrieking like a five-year-old. As our car speeds down one of the hills in the track, Jan's seat restraint suddenly snaps open and she's hurled out of the car. I see her shooting like a missile through the air and know it's going to kill her. I feel relieved.

When I woke up, I was shocked at my lack of emotion and couldn't go back to sleep. But the longer I lay there, the clearer it became that she and I no longer enjoyed the same things, that she was immature, and that for me the relationship was already over. Ending it was merely a formality.

★ ★ ★

Prophetic Death Dream

Author Anne Rice, while speaking one year at the Miami Book Fair, told the heartbreaking story of how she had come to write *Interview with the Vampire*.

She had dreamed that her young daughter was dying of a blood disease. Shortly afterward, the girl was diagnosed with leukemia. In the aftermath of her daughter's death, Rice wrote *Vampire* in a feverish frenzy in just three weeks, as though it were a kind of purging. It's probably no coincidence that blood is the theme of the book.

In the next dream, a hillside was the setting for a glimpse of a young man's death.

★ ★ ★

THE HILLSIDE

John and I are sitting on a grassy hillside overlooking a valley. I'm not real sure what we're doing here or how we came to be here, but that doesn't seem to matter in the dream. We're talking about people we knew in college and the crazy things we did. Suddenly he turns to me and says, "It's time for me to move on. But don't worry about me. I'll be in touch."

The next morning, I remembered dreaming about him and figured the dream meant he would be showing up any day now. He was nomadic in that sense, taking off when he felt like it, hitching around the country and dropping in on friends, who were always glad to see him. I kept thinking that I should call our mutual friend, Linda, who usually knew where he was.

But that evening, Linda called me in tears. John had been killed in a car accident the night before.

★ ★ ★

Several years later, the woman dreamed that she and John met on the same hillside, talking and laughing again about old times. Then he suddenly turned to her and said he was "moving on to the next level." She hasn't dreamed of him in the more than twenty years since.

In the case of John and the hillside dream, there was nothing the dreamer could do to prevent the death. But some near-death dreams do exactly that. You dream, for example, that the plane you're supposed to take tomorrow crashes and because of the dream, you change your flight. Later, you hear that the plane crashed.

COUSIN, AUNT, UNCLE

To dream of members of your extended family is not always portentous. To dream of a cousin indicates you might have disappointment and sadness. Even dreaming of a friendly correspondence with your cousin signifies that there might be a major falling-out in the family.

If a woman dreams of her aunt, she will soon receive severe criticism of choices and actions she makes in life. And if a man or woman dreams of an uncle, beware, sad news will soon reach you.

Best not to dream about your extended family. Send them a card instead!

But a dream doesn't have to prophesy death in order for you to benefit from it. In Seth's view of things, you might, for example, oversleep the next morning and miss the plane. Or you might take a route to the airport that plunges you headlong into a traffic jam and, thus, miss your flight. In the latter case, a series of synchronicities would save your life, but the source would still be the dream you had the night before.

Dreams of Death as Other-Dimensional

Only rarely do death dreams portend an actual physical death. In the following dream, which deals with the living and the dead, the dream is more about the woman's future life than her death.

Laura, a forty-five-year-old woman, had asked for a dream to confirm that things in her life were "clicking along" as they should be. She had the following dream:

★ ★ ★

COMMUNITY THEATER

I'm in a barnlike structure, perhaps a community theater. Both the living and the dead are here, as though this is some sort of meeting place between worlds or dimensions. A woman informs me that by punching in my birth data information, I can find out anything about myself or my life that I need to know.

There are people here who travel about in both the world of the living and the world of the dead. One such woman tells me that one day the "glass" between the borders of life and death will be so clear that you'll be able to "see" through it.

The dream ends with a fire drill. My former headmistress sticks her head inside and orders everyone to get outside.

★ ★ ★

The dreamer was an amateur astrologer, so the birth date reference made sense to her. She interpreted it as a message to do a progressed astrological chart on herself for the coming year. She also felt this was a clear message from her unconscious that everything she needed to know was available to her in the dream state; all she had to do was ask. It reassured her that her unconscious was always accessible and that she already possessed tools in her waking life to clarify issues and questions.

When she related the dream to her husband, he replied that the birth data reference sounded like a computerized akashic record, the "cosmic" records that noted seer Edgar Cayce supposedly accessed during his readings. The dreamer felt that the "glass" that separates the living and the dead was the dream state. The fire drill at the end of the dream is literally a wake-up call, prodding her to consciousness so she'll record the dream.

Exercise 9: DREAMS ABOUT DEATH

Describe four death dreams and their outcomes. List any dreams about death that you've had that you can recall. Describe them in as much detail as you remember. Then describe the meaning of the dream: Was it a signal of a personal transformation or an actual warning of death?

Dream 1: ....

....

....

....

....

Dream 2: ....

....

....

....

....

Dream 3: ....

....

....

....

....

Dream 4: ....

....

....

....

....

CHICKENS, ROOSTER, HEN, TURKEY

Everyone eats tons of chicken, or so it seems, so why not dream about chickens? To dream of a brood of chickens denotes that you have worries from many cares, but some of that worry you will profit from. And if you dream of young chicks, you will be very successful in all your enterprises.

To dream of a rooster also means you will be successful and rise to places of great honor. To dream of hens means you will attend a pleasant family reunion.

To dream of a turkey also denotes good luck to come your way, especially abundant gains in business. To dream of eating turkey indicates you will be attending a happy, bounteous occasion—like a Thanksgiving celebration!

Death Dreams Involving Relatives or Family Members

A death or near-death dream involving a family member or relative, like most death dreams, may point to a major upheaval in that person's life. The dream acts as a conduit of information, as in the next example.

APPARITION

Aunt Pat, my mother's older sister, appears to me, hovering like a ghost in a corner of the bedroom. In the dream, the image is so clear I can see the lines in her face, the soft gray of her hair, the shape of her mouth.

She's speaking to me, but I can't hear the words.

I suddenly associate this kind of apparition with stories I've heard about people who appear to loved ones at the time of their death. I try to scream, but can't, and bolt awake. For seconds it seems that the image of my aunt is actually in a corner of the bedroom, exactly where it was in the dream. Then I blink and the apparition fades. Or maybe it wasn't really there at all; maybe I imagined it. I still don't know.

The next day, I called my parents and asked if my aunt was okay. As far as they knew she was. I forgot about the dream until several days later, when my parents said they'd spoken to my aunt. She had fallen and cracked her hip over the same weekend I had

the dream and was planning on moving in with her son.

★ ★ ★

Despite immediate evidence to the contrary, this dream indicated that the aunt would be or already was undergoing a major life change.

HELPFUL SEX DREAMS

Sex dream stories can be immensely helpful in recognizing and overcoming inhibitions to fulfillment and intimacy. If you've had a sex dream in which one or both of your parents have appeared, here are some questions you can ask yourself:

Is there some belief, fear, or expectation you learned from your parent(s) that tends to intrude into your awareness as you begin to make love?

Is there a sense in which you believe your fulfillment might be disloyal or damaging to your parents?

Were you more worried about your parent(s) presence than about your sexual fulfillment? If so, do you worry about their opinions more than is objectively necessary?

Sex Dreams

Sex and *dreams* and *Freud*—the three words seem intricately linked. According to Sigmund Freud, all of our dreams are linked with sexual issues. Freud was writing during the Victorian era, when talk of sex was taboo, and his ideas helped free the Western world from the repressive strictures of the era.

However, his view that the sex drive powered virtually all of our dreams is no longer accepted. In fact, it's now thought by some dream researchers that some sex dreams may not have anything to do with sex.

Erotica

Erotic dreams have heightened physical sensation and are often sexually satisfying. They can be very graphic, like an X-rated movie, and the sexual activity can be the main or only action within the dream plot. These dreams may be the mind's attempt to satisfy the natural sexual appetite, and they can be influenced by all sorts of stimuli, such as erotic novels or movies.

Erotic dreams can be compared with eating rich chocolate without calories; there's no risk, no involvement, and no consequences. They fall into the category of what Freud referred to as wish fulfillment.

★ ★ ★

IN BED WITH PAUL NEWMAN

Paul Newman walks into my bedroom. He looks like he did in Cool Hand Luke. He smiles—you know that smile. And he knows me. There's nothing awkward about our meeting. In the blink of an eye, we're making passionate love. It seems to go on a long time and he's very intimate, tender, and caring with me. It's a very fulfilling experience.

★ ★ ★

The dreamer, Elaine, dreamed of Paul Newman after seeing one of his movies. Even though Newman is about twenty-five years older than Elaine, she has admired him since she was a teenager and still considers him sexy. Such sex dreams can fulfill a fantasy or enhance your love life.

Dreams in which you are making love to a famous person can also be related to your desire to achieve success in the world in which the famous person has starred. A budding writer may dream of sleeping with a best-selling author, a struggling athlete may dream of marrying a well-known professional athlete, and a beginning television reporter may dream of sleeping with a famous broadcaster.

Sexual dreams can also contain clues to important personal needs, desires, fears, and changes.

Exercise 10: SEX DREAMS AND RELATIONSHIPS

You may have had a sex dream that you think concerns patterns of your relationships. This exercise can help you understand the meaning of the dream and learn from it.

What is the dream telling you about your past or present partner(s)?

What is the dream telling you about yourself?

Are you frustrated with difficulties in finding a permanent partner?

Do you find that your relationships begin in a promising manner and then just fall apart?

What is the significant pattern that the dream reveals?

Do you look at your partner through "rose-colored glasses" until you become close to him or her?

Do you jump too quickly into a relationship?

Were you too critical of past lovers?

Does your lover take advantage of you? Did your past lovers take advantage of you?

ECSTASY, JOY, PLEASURE, MERRY DELIGHT

To dream of happiness means happy events will occur in your life. To dream of ecstasy, that feeling of overwhelming, rapturous delight, portends you will have a visit from a long, absent friend.

Dreaming of joy—feeling of well-being and good fortune—means that there will be harmony among all your friends.

A dream about pleasure—feeling of gratification—means you will have many financial and personal gains of enjoyment.

To dream of being merry, full of gaiety and high spirits, means that pleasant events and affairs will soon prove profitable.

Dreaming about being in a state of delight, that is to feel keen enjoyment, means also that all aspects of your life will go well and you will be successful.

The message is clear, dream of being happy and you will be happy!

OTHER SEX DREAM THEMES

You may recognize a familiar theme in some of the following sexual dreams. You and your dreams are unique, so think of these interpretations as starting points, not conclusions.

Searching for a place to make love. You search from house to house, town to town. The dream is more about the search for a place than about sex itself. Such dreams are a metaphor for a search for intimacy.

Making love, but stopping short of climax. In this dream, you're left unfulfilled. It starts out promising, but just fizzles out, leaving you frustrated and angry. This dream symbolizes a lack of fulfillment and a frustration in life that may have nothing at all to do with your sex life. Look at recent events in your life. What has left you frustrated?

Making love in a public place. Your performance is observed by others. This dream dramatically calls your attention to a public action in your life. What is it that you recently did in public or are about to do? Take a close look at the event. Look at other aspects of the dream. Who is your partner? How is that person involved in the public event in your waking life? If the person has no connection with the event, then what does that person symbolize?

People recovering from illness, depression, surgery, or the grieving process, for example, may suddenly and inexplicably begin having erotic dreams. Such dreams appear to be associated with an increase in physical vitality and a greater sense of aliveness, although they may precede physical recovery in some cases. The dreamer is often struck with the humor of the situation, considering his or her recent physical challenges. Yet, these dreams serve as reminders that although you've been through hell, you're still very much alive.

Sexual Inhibitions

A common dream that deals with sexual inhibitions is one in which one or both of your parents walk in on you while you are making love. In such a dream, your parent might talk to you as if there is nothing unusual about his or her appearance in your bedroom. An important aspect of the dream is the identity of your partner. If it's your spouse, consider whether your parents approve of your spouse, or whether you feel a need for such approval. But there are also other scenarios, as the one that follows.

★　★　★

PARENTS AND SEX DREAMS

In the dream, I'm making love with this attractive guy who works in my office. Everything is going great until I see my mother standing over the bed. I jerk the sheet over my lover, and I demand to know what she's doing in my bedroom. She doesn't answer, but she has a disapproving expression on her face. She simply turns and marches out of the room.

★ ★ ★

For Julie, the dream was easy to interpret. She found the man attractive and liked being around him. But she also loved her husband and wouldn't get involved with the man in her waking life. Her mother's appearance suggested to her that she felt guilty about her attraction to another man. "If you find yourself enjoying sex in a dream in circumstances your waking mind finds shocking, this is a sure sign that you are imposing a lifestyle on yourself which is at variance with your natural feelings in some way, and your dream is a warning to change it," says Ann Faraday in *The Dream Game*. "The most important thing . . . is to become aware of one's own feelings, thereby avoiding the danger of the repressed impulses seeking expression in some devious way, perhaps by outbursts of anger against one's partner or by 'accidentally' finding oneself in some compromising situation with the dream lover in waking life."

Relationships

Many sexual dreams are a commentary on your past and present relationships. These dreams often feature past lovers. In the most outrageous ones, all of your past lovers show up at the same party or in the same bed. The function of this dream seems to be to help analyze past involvements that continue to impact current relationships.

It's important to look for patterns that mark your relationships. This is especially important if you've had a series of unsuccessful relationships or affairs that began filled with promise and ended badly.

Here's a dream with a different plot, but a similar theme. The dreamer, Bill, was a thirty-three-year-old engineer who had never been married.

★ ★ ★

THE VANISHING LOVER

Everything starts out great. I'm with Sharon, a woman I've known through business for several months. I'm very attracted to her and now we're in a romantic setting. We both know what we want and neither of us has any inhibitions. But just as I become fully aroused, Sharon starts to disappear. All of my efforts to keep her from vanishing fail. Sharon simply evaporates.

★ ★ ★

For Bill, the meaning of the dream is more about a pattern in his life than a statement about Sharon. He has rarely had a sexual relationship last longer than a few months. Part of Bill's problem, he admits, is that he only likes the exciting early sexual encounters with a new mate. Once the woman starts to become part of his life, his interest fades.

CHAPTER TEN

More Common Dream Themes

There are certain dream themes that seem to be common to many of us.

The themes probably don't qualify as archetypal; that is, they are not *forces* within us. Their genesis usually lies in our daily lives and experiences. Sometimes, they express fears or anxieties; other times, they express joy or triumph. In all cases, though, they tell us what is on our minds and in our hearts, so they deserve attention.

These common themes are frequently found in recurring dreams, which may mean that you're stuck in a particular pattern or that some issue hasn't been resolved. Once you begin working with your dreams, though, their content will probably change.

Some of the most common themes include the following:

☆ Falling

☆ Flying

☆ An examination for which you're unprepared

☆ Attending a class

☆ Being nude

> *Then suddenly I detach myself from the windowsill on which I am lying, and in the same reclining position fly slowly over the lane, over the houses, and then over the Golden Horn in the direction of Stamboul.*
>
> — P.D. OUSPENSKY,
> *A NEW MODEL OF THE UNIVERSE*

☆ Losing keys, a wallet, a purse, or a briefcase

☆ Taking a bus, train, or plane

☆ Having your teeth fall out

☆ Finding money

This is by no means a definitive list. Themes, like societies themselves, undoubtedly change over time. For the children of today, new themes may include UFOs and/or alien abductions; a computer system crash; extreme weather; airplane disasters; or other popular media topics.

Falling

Dreams of falling may be metaphors for the *fallen* woman, a *fall* from grace, or the *fall* season. The interpretation depends, to a large extent, on what is going on in your life at the time or what happened to you within the twenty-four hours preceding the dream.

One young married woman's dream that she was falling from a building struck her as a metaphor for her affair with a married man from her office. The fall, she said, didn't just represent a fall from grace; it was also a metaphor for what would happen to her marriage if her husband discovered the affair.

Quite often such a dream will have that "zing" to it and you'll know immediately what it's referring to. But other times, its meaning may be as obscure as a Rubik's cube. You'll have to take it apart piece by piece, then figure out how to put it back together.

Dream therapist Gayle Delaney suggests that you ask yourself how you feel as you're falling. Do you feel terrified? Helpless? Out of control? Or is the sensation pleasant? If so, how?

Derek, an actor, dreamed he was in a convertible with his agent, who was driving. While they were speeding along a country road, the car hit a deep hole and veered out of control. His agent, a woman, slammed her foot on the brake, but the brakes failed and they plunged over the side of a cliff.

There are many possible interpretations of this dream. But the only one that mattered was the one that made sense to Derek, that offered him new insight into his relationship with his agent. He mulled the dream over for a day or two, and realized that for quite a while he'd felt as if she had mishandled his career and wasn't able to *apply the brake* to

this downward spiral. He ended their partnership several days later, a split that was, for him, like a plunge over the edge of a cliff, into an abyss of the unknown.

Flying

Freud connected flying in a dream with the desire for sex. Alfred Adler connected these dreams with the will to dominate others. And Carl Jung saw them as the desire to break free of restrictions. Most psychotherapists today tend to favor Jung's interpretation.

But like other dreams, it's best to look at flying dreams as individual experiences. To that end, ask yourself whether the sensation of flying is pleasurable or stressful. Why are you flying? Are you escaping pursuers? Are you showing off? Or do you feel elated? Is it merely something you're able to do? As with any of these common dream themes, explore your feelings about the dream and the action that takes place. Does it seem familiar, as if you've been flying before?

Some flying dreams may involve out-of-body travel, a topic that is explored in detail in part three of this book. These experiences have a distinctly different feel to them, however, and often involve "travel" to places both familiar and strange.

In the following dream, Ken, a forty-two-year-old insurance adjuster, who is an avid runner, recalled a flying dream that related to running. In a sense, it was a step beyond running.

Exercise 11: MY FALLING DREAM

Jot down a recurring falling dream you've had. If it was recent, note what was going on in your life at the time of the dream. Had you reached a crossroad in a relationship? Was an important partnership in the throes of change? Had your kids recently left home? Did you have a drug or an alcohol habit? Interpret the dream. Note if a decision was made as a result of this dream. Let the dream speak to you.

Date: .... Time: ....

The dream: ....

....

....

....

....

....

....

....

Events immediately preceding the dream: ....

....

....

....

....

Interpretation: ....

....

....

....

....

....

....

Remarks: ....

....

....

....

....

RUNNING TO FLY

I'm running in a field and my body is getting lighter with each stride. My steps lengthen and pretty soon I pick up speed. Then I'm airborne, I'm soaring, it's exhilarating. Then it occurs to me that I've done this before. "It's easy," I think. "Nothing to it." I tell myself I have to remember that I know how to fly.

I was excited when I woke from the dream. It took a few minutes before I realized I'd been dreaming and that I couldn't really fly in my waking life.

Ken looked at his flying dream as a symbol of accomplishment. The day of the dream he had placed second in his age bracket and twelfth overall in a local 10 kilometer race with more than seven hundred contestants. After the race, he felt elevated, and that sensation was transformed into his dream.

Examinations

Jim, a self-employed contractor, dreamed that he was hurrying to make an 8 a.m. class. When he got there, the professor was passing out final exam booklets. He realized that he'd been to the class only a couple of times the entire semester and that he wasn't prepared for the exam.

Although it had been more than twenty years since Jim had graduated from college, he had this dream once or twice a year. The specifics rarely changed. Once he began to record and study his dreams, however, he understood that the dream usually occurred when he was facing a bid on a major project. Even though he spent weeks preparing figures on a prospective project, he rarely felt adequately prepared.

For most of us, the examination dream follows a format similar to Jim's. Ann Faraday, in *Dream Game,* notes that most of these dreams occur when we feel we're being "tested" or "examined" by someone, as during a job interview, for example, or perhaps in some area of our spiritual lives.

All of us have felt unprepared at one time or another, and the examination dream is often a reflection of the uneasy sensation of not being ready for something coming into our lives. But again, the only interpretation that matters is your own.

When interpreting this type of dream, make note of whether you're under a deadline or extreme pressure in your waking life. If you're not, then ask whether there is something in your life that you feel unprepared to cope with. In your dream journal, record the dream as you did in Exercises 11 and 12.

Classrooms

When you dream of finding yourself in a classroom, examine your surroundings and your reason for being there. Is there a posi-

Exercise 12: MY FLYING DREAM

Note a recurring flying dream you've had. You may want to reserve a section in your journal to record recurring dreams. In this way, over a period of time, you'll see whether or how the content of the dreams change.

Date: .... Time: ....

The dream: ....

....

....

....

....

....

....

....

Events immediately preceding the dream: ....

....

....

....

....

Interpretation: ....

....

....

....

....

Remarks: ....

....

....

....

....

tive feeling about the learning environment? Do you recognize who is teaching the class and the subject matter? Oftentimes, a classroom dream relates to a personal growth period you are going through.

The following classroom dream was told by a thirty-three-year-old woman who had recently joined a dream group. The dream had occurred eleven years earlier, when she was in college, and it had always puzzled her. She asked if anyone in the dream group had any idea of what it meant. As you read through this dream, take special note of the way the woman describes the "lobby" and classroom.

★   ★   ★

ORIENTATION

Tanya and I are sitting in a lobby with perhaps a dozen other people of various ages and races. We aren't sure why we're there. There's nothing about the lobby to tell me exactly where it is. I feel very uneasy about this place. I go up to the information desk and ask the receptionist what we're waiting for.

"For the class to begin," she replies.

"I didn't sign up for a class," I tell her.

"You must have. You're here."

Then she goes back to whatever she was doing, and I return to my seat. Not long afterward, she calls my name and Tanya's and we file into a college-style auditorium. It's crowded with people and brightly lit by a skylight. The color of

the sky is odd, a kind of glowing cerulean blue.

The speaker is a well-known literary figure (whose name I forgot when I woke), but who I know died some years before. I suddenly realize I am in an afterlife classroom, about to be oriented to dying and to whatever happens next.

★   ★   ★

Several members of the dream group immediately associated the dream with reports from near-death survivors. The dreamer herself agreed, but pointed out that no one had died around the time she'd had the dream and that she had never had a near-death experience. In fact, at the time of the dream, Raymond Moody's seminal book on near-death experiences, *Life After Death,* hadn't yet been published. But the dream confirmed her belief in the survival of consciousness and triggered a lifelong interest in metaphysical topics.

The dream recurs periodically, usually when the woman experiences a "crisis of faith" in her spiritual beliefs. It always renews her belief in the path she has chosen.

When a teacher has a classroom dream, the meaning might be more practical than symbolic. That was the case in the following dream related by Bharata, the fifty-one-year-old director of the Sivananda Yoga Center in Lake Worth, Florida. He dreamed that he was the only teacher for two classes which were scheduled to meet at the same time,

Eye, Eyebrows, One-eyed Cyclops

B eware of dreaming of one eye—it portends that watchful enemies will ferret out a chance to do you harm in your business. Dreaming of a one-eyed man indicates loss and trouble with others plotting against you in your business.

If you dream in color, and most people do, and you dream of brown eyes, it denotes there is deceit and treachery in your life. If you dream of blue eyes, it denotes you are weak in carrying out your intentions. Dreaming of gray eyes mean you love flattery.

All and all dreaming of eyes usually portends bad news. If you dream of losing an eye or sore eye, watch out for trouble.

and he had to teach both classes, running back and forth from room to room.

In Bharata's case, the classroom dream was a reflection of his inner concern that he was teaching too many classes. Although he enjoyed teaching, his schedule included two or three classes a day and he had been considering adding other teachers.

Nudity

A nudity dream draws your attention like few others. Finding oneself naked in a public place, such as on a busy street, is embarrassing. If you've had such an experience, you probably were relieved when you realized that it was a dream. The first reaction to such a dream might be to consider its practical implications. If you are about to embark on a trip and dreamed of being naked while traveling, check your luggage to make sure you're taking everything you need.

But like other common dreams, the nudity is more likely symbolic. You are exposed. That can be good or bad. Are you looking for exposure, for example, to publicize something you've done? Or, are you hiding something from the public that you've done? In either case, a nudity dream brings to light a concern. Or it could suggest that the exposure that you've been seeking is about to occur.

Ann Faraday in *The Dream Game* tells of a young man's dream of being naked in front of a cheering crowd. In waking life, he

had recently had his first experience of sexual intercourse, and for him the dream meant that he had shed his moral prohibitions. "Had the onlookers in the dream been disapproving, this would have indicated guilt feelings, for in the objective world, his fellow students would certainly have approved," Faraday wrote.

Lost Purse, Wallet, Keys, or Briefcase

Purses and wallets usually contain credit cards, money, and identification—society's evidence of who you are. Keys open doors, start cars, and allow us entrance to our homes and offices. Briefcases typically contain papers related to work. Therefore, says Gayle Delaney, this dream usually occurs among women whose kids have recently left home and among men who have retired or who have been fired from their jobs. Such dreams have also been reported by people who are in the midst of transition from one way of life or mode of thought to another. It has to do with a shift in identity.

Taking a Bus, Train, or Plane

Dreaming of travel could relate to an upcoming trip. But if you have no plans for a

FLOWERS

■

To dream of a wreath of fresh flowers denotes that great opportunity will come your way. You'll have great success if you chose to take advantage of that opportunity.

But if you dream of a bier, which are the flowers on a coffin, no matter how fresh and beautiful the flowers are, you will know losses. Happier circumstances are denoted by dreaming of bouquets, especially if they are made up of richly colored flowers. A legacy from an unknown and wealthy relative will soon be yours. In addition there will probably be a pleasant gathering of young folks in your life.

Exercise 13: MY RECURRING DREAMS

Categorize three of your recurring dreams under broad topic headings like the ones presented in this chapter. Then, just as you did in Exercise 4, define what these symbols mean to you in your waking life. Do the definitions fit the dreams?

If these are recent dreams and you've recorded them in your journal, read them over and note what was going on in your life at the time you had the dreams. Then interpret the dreams.

Broad categories and meanings:

What was going on in my life at the time of these dreams?

Dream 1

Dream 2

Dream 3

Interpretation of dreams:

Dream 1

Dream 2

Dream 3

Notes

journey, your dream sojourn may be a symbolic one. Pay particular attention to details about your trip. Where are you going? Are you traveling alone or with others? Do you have luggage with you? Keep in mind that what happens on your trip might be more important than the destination.

The following dream was told by a newspaper reporter named Jerry. He cited a recurring dream related to travel and missed connections

MISSING CONNECTIONS

I'm taking a train in a foreign country and must transfer from one train to another. The problem is that I've lost track of my luggage. I'm looking all over for it, and I know I must hurry or I'll miss the connecting train. Sometimes

I'm in a train station without my luggage, which is still on the train I just got off. I usually wake up before I find out what happens.

After discussing the dream with friends, Jerry saw two possible meanings for the dream. In both of them, the journey was his job. Although he didn't travel much, his work relied on making connections with sources for stories. His fear was that he wouldn't make contact with his sources or that when he reached them, he wouldn't be ready for the interview. His luggage represented his preparation for the interview.

The other interpretation involved the question of his future as a reporter. Jerry was tired of chasing down stories day after day and wanted to make a career change.

But he feared that he was not prepared to make the change—that he would "miss his connection" to a new career.

Losing Teeth

A dream about losing teeth might be a literal warning about your dental condition. But if you've had a checkup, then you should consider that the dream might be telling you something about yourself.

Ann Faraday notes that her own loss-of-teeth dreams "almost always reflect my feeling that I have 'lost face' or 'spoiled my self-image' in some way during the day, usually by giving in to emotions of fear or weakness." Edgar Cayce viewed dreams of losing teeth as metaphors for loose or careless speech.

However, if those meanings don't work for you, ask yourself what teeth mean to you. Do they represent power? A nice appearance? Aggressiveness? What is it that makes you feel "toothless"?

Finding Money

Another common dream involves finding money. Sometimes the money is in the form of coins and they are in the ground. The deeper you dig, the more coins you find. If you find the coins in the roots of a tree, think about how roots are the hidden strength of a tree—without them the tree dies.

Terri, the woman who related the next dream, grew up listening to her father say that money "doesn't grow on trees." It seemed that every time she wanted something, her father replied with that well-worn phrase.

THE MONEY TREE

I'm digging for something under a large tree. I can feel the dirt under my nails; the scent of the earth fills me. I find one coin, and then several more. The deeper I dig, the more money I find. I feel excited, as though I've just discovered some wonderful secret—that money really does grow on trees!

For Terri, money still doesn't grow on trees, but if you dig deep within, you'll find hidden riches. Such dreams don't necessarily refer to money, but rather to the riches within. The inner self roots us to our true nature, and therein lies an abundance of riches, which are often greater than we realize.

PART THREE

The Far Side
of Dreaming

Ask any three-year-old about his or her nightmares and you'll probably hear of dreams in which the child was pursued by terrifying animals—monkeys that grinned, dragons, wolves, huge dogs, or lions.

Common Themes and Symbols

Quite often, children's nightmares occur after a scolding or punishment by parents. Or they occur when a child is ill or in transition, for example, during a divorce or a move from one home to another. Sometimes they occur for no apparent external reason. By gently interviewing children about their nightmares, you can usually get to the source of what caused them.

As children near the age of six, their nightmares change. Instead of pursuit and threats by animals, the bad guy may be a bully in the class or down the street. These nightmares often deal with anxieties and

> *Into what nightmare of thingness am I fallen?*
>
> — SAMUEL BECKETT,
> *THE CALMATIVE*

fears in children's waking lives. This pattern can also be true of adults, but once you're grown, nightmares become somewhat more complicated.

In *The Bedside Guide to Dreams,* Stase Michaels outlines three different kinds of nightmares that are common to adults. "In the first kind, you face your actual fears. In the second, you deal with the pain and trauma in yourself and in your life. The third kind is the most common type of dream and is reflected in the saying 'I have met the enemy, and it is I.'"

In the third kind of nightmare, you encounter a part of yourself that you would rather not see. In waking life, this kind of encounter is what Brugh Joy calls "reactive"—your reaction to someone or something is extreme compared with the reality of the situation. You may respond with a loud objection, criticism, anger, or righteous indignation, although the source of your reaction is nearly always within yourself. The person or event you're reacting to hits an all too familiar chord because it reflects some element in yourself that you would rather keep hidden.

Often, these nightmares seem to be a literal warning about something—your health, your car, a pending accident, or a neighborhood to avoid. But before you

HOME, AMERICA, ASIA, EUROPE

I f you dream of places, it's best to dream of a village. To dream of a village means you will enjoy good health and will be provided for in your lifetime.

To dream of the United States as a nation, such as taking a voyage to the United States, take care. Trouble might be around the corner. If you dream of traveling to Asia, a change will happen in your life from which you will derive no material benefits. If you dream of traveling to Europe, you soon will go on a long journey, but this long journey will greatly increase your finances. Get packed!

jump to any conclusions about your nightmare being a literal warning, exhaust the other possibilities.

Look for metaphors. Scrutinize the dream for hints that it illuminates some part of your personality you don't want to know about. Be honest. Does it depict one of your actual fears? Does it address a rejected part of yourself?

If the nightmare doesn't seem to fall into any of the other categories, then Michaels suggests that it might be a true warning, and that you should look for the following:

Vividness. Warning dreams are usually very vivid.

Your reactions. How you react in a warning dream is how you would react in waking life to the same situation or event.

Duplication of details. In a warning dream, your house looks like the actual house you live in. Your mother looks like your real mother. There is a literal feel to the dream that is lacking in the other kinds of dreams.

In the nightmare that follows, the dreamer was living on the first floor of a condominium complex. Although the complex was safe, the neighborhood outside of it was one of the worst in town. Many people in the complex had security systems in their condos and in their cars. The dreamer didn't. The only thing that stood between her and the outside world were dead bolts.

★ ★ ★

DEAD BOLT

I'm in the kitchen in the middle of the night, getting something to eat. Only the light over the stove is on. The door, which opens onto the condo courtyard, begins to rattle and I whip around. A horrible paralysis seizes me. I can't move or scream. I can only watch.

A hand reaches inside the door. A man's hand. I can see the dirt under his fingernails. He is trying to reach the chain. I grab the tea kettle and slam it against his fingers. His hand vanishes.

I am looking at a broken dead bolt. I kick the door shut and fix a chair in front of it. I awaken in my bedroom, certain the man is out there in the courtyard now, and that he's going to try to break into the condo—my condo.

★ ★ ★

Here, the dreamer is being warned about the broken dead bolt in her kitchen door. She admits that right after she had the dream, she hired a locksmith to come out to the condo and fix the door. For some time, the dead bolt had been broken and the entire locking mechanism could be slipped out of the door, providing a peephole to the outside world.

This dream possessed a vividness the dreamer recognized. It was also quite literal:

Exercise 14: CONFRONTING MY FEAR

Analyze one of your recurring nightmares. What are the prevalent images? Where does the dream take place? Are there any obvious metaphors or puns that may hold a vital clue to the meaning of the dream? How does the dream end? If you've never confronted your fear in this nightmare, rewrite the ending of the dream so that you do.

The nightmare: ....
....
....
....
....
....
....
....

Setting: ....
....
....
....

Metaphors: ....
....
....

How I act/react in the dream: ....
....
....
....
....
....

How I would change this dream: ....
....
....
....

Her kitchen was depicted as it actually was, the dead bolt on the kitchen door was definitely broken, and the intruder's hand was rendered in astonishing detail. Two weeks later, a condo three doors down from hers was broken into.

Confronting Your Fear

When a Senoi child is frightened in a dream, he's advised to confront the fear. He is encouraged to call on dream friends to help him, but if he's attacked, he's supposed to retaliate. Only then will his attacker leave him alone.

". . . to confront and conquer danger," writes Patricia Garfield, "is the most important rule in the Senoi system of dream control."

Some of us stumble on this rule without ever having heard about the Senoi. After one woman was raped, she had repeated dreams in which the rapist was chasing her. Finally, in the following dream, she seized control of the situation.

★ ★ ★

THE RAPIST
The scene was the same as in the other dreams, the man chasing me down a dark alley between a pair of brownstone buildings. I'm so terrified the inside of my mouth is bone dry. I can see the end of the alley just ahead, can see lights, traffic, but I know I'm not going to make it.

So I suddenly stop, turn, and demand that he leave me alone. He looks at me for a long moment, then holds out his hand. I can see something in his palm, but I don't want to approach him to take it. I tell him to drop it on the ground and he does. Then he walks away from me, whistling.

When he's gone, I walk over to where he was standing and find a beautiful, pink shell—the object he dropped. It has my name on it. I've never had the dream since.

★ ★ ★

Exercise 15: MY WAKING FEARS

List five of your fears. Have any of these fears shown up in your dreams? Were they couched in metaphorical images? Make note of how you dealt with these fears in your dreams. Then, outline a plan for conquering these fears in your waking life.

List your fears and note if they have appeared in your dreams:

Fear 1 ....

....

....

Fear 2 ....

....

....

Fear 3 ....

....

....

Fear 4 ....

....

....

Fear 5 ....

....

....

How would you overcome these fears in your waking life? What steps would you take?

Step 1 ....

....

Step 2 ....

....

Step 3 ....

....

Step 4 ....

....

Step 5 ....

....

HANDKERCHIEFS

Most people don't carry cloth handkerchiefs today, availing themselves of tissues, but if you should dream of a handkerchief, it means you will embark on a flirtatious affair. That's good news if you are single.

If you dream of losing a handkerchief, it indicates a broken engagement will possibly occur. A torn handkerchief portends you will have a lovers quarrel, and a reconciliation will be impossible. To dream of silk handkerchiefs is much better. It denotes that your pleasing and magnetic personality will make an auspicious existence for yourself.

The woman interpreted the shell as a womb, which serves as a protective shelter for a fetus. In this case, the shell was a symbol of protection, which the woman had gained for herself.

Night Terrors

You've just turned out the light and are settling in for a good night's sleep when a bloodcurdling scream shreds the silence. You leap up and rush into your son's room and find him in a total panic, completely disoriented. When you calm him down and question him, he tells you about a single, horrifying image of being crushed or strangled or attacked.

It isn't a nightmare that woke him, but night terrors, which are most common in children between the ages of three and eight. Most kids either remember nothing about what frightened them or recall only fragmented images, which is characteristic of what happens when you're awakened from the deepest stages of sleep.

Ernest Hartmann, a psychoanalyst and author of *The Nightmare,* says that night terrors sometimes run in families, suggesting that there may be a genetic susceptibility to them. It's not known why some people don't grow out of night terrors, but he adds, "Some adults with night terrors have been noted to have phobic or obsessional personalities.

There is sometimes a sense that these people are unable or unwilling to notice or express strong feelings in the daytime; in them, the night terror episodes may express a kind of outbreak of repressed emotion."

Your Waking Fears

Most people don't obsess about the things or situations they fear. They simply react when confronted with the fear. But by consciously recognizing what you fear, you take the first step to overcoming it. Lynn, a thirty-year-old mother and photographer, was absolutely petrified of snakes until she got a photography assignment that took her to the Miami serpentarium.

"Maybe it was seeing them through the lens of the camera. Maybe it was just that I was ready to deal with the fear. But suddenly, I recognized their beauty, their incredible diversity. Toward the end of the assignment, one of the snake handlers brought over a boa he had worked with since it was born. I actually mustered the courage to touch it. And from that point on, I was no longer afraid of snakes."

CHAPTER TWELVE

Out-of-Body
Dreams

One Sunday after-noon in 1958, Robert Monroe, a Virginia businessman and electronic engineer, laid down on the couch for a short nap. His body began to shake violently, but he couldn't move. Terrified, he finally forced himself to sit upright on the couch. The vibration faded away and he stood up and walked around.

This experience was repeated a number of times during the ensuing months. Monroe thought there was something physically wrong, like epilepsy or a brain tumor, but his family doctor gave him a clean bill of health.

Monroe committed himself to exploring the sensation, which continued to occur over the next few months. Then one night when the vibrations started up, Monroe realized he could move his fingers. His arm was draped over the side of the bed and his fingers were brushing the rug, so he pressed down with his fingertips. His fingers seemed to penetrate the rug, so he pressed down harder and his hand sank into the floor.

He returned to his doctor, who advised him to lose some weight, smoke less, and to look into yoga. Some practitioners of yoga,

> *All that we see or seem is but a dream within a dream.*
>
> —EDGAR ALLAN POE,
> *A DREAM WITHIN A DREAM*

the doctor said, claimed they could travel out of their bodies at will. The very notion struck Monroe as absurd. The vibrations came and went six more times before he mustered the nerve to explore. Then, one night, with the vibrations in full force, he thought of floating upward—and did.

For Monroe, this was the beginning of a lifelong exploration into out-of-body travel. He wrote three books on his experiences and started the Monroe Institute, a research and educational facility. At the Institute, people are taught how to travel out of their bodies and to objectively gather information in these inner realms, using "maps" and "landmarks" that Monroe charted during his thousands of out-of-body experiences, (OBEs).

OBEs and flying dreams are quite often related. Earlier we looked at flying dreams from a symbolic perspective; however, it's also worthwhile to consider their relationship to OBEs.

Flying During Dreams

Some people report that to fly in a dream, all they have to do is flap their arms. Other

INHERITANCE, DISINHERITANCE

Dreaming you come into an inheritance naturally indicates good things will happen in your life. In fact dreaming of inheriting money denotes that you will be successful and very easily obtain the rest of your dreams.

Dreaming of disinheritance of course denotes loss and rough times. But if you dream of a will or of making your will, possibly momentous trials and speculations will occur in your life.

people have to take off at a run, sort of like Superman. In some flying dreams, you simply lift off the ground and drift on the currents of air. In still others, you only have to think of a place in order to experience a sensation of tremendous speed and momentum.

Flying dreams vary from one person to another. For some people, the experience is joyous and related to freedom from the normal confines of the physical body. For others, flying dreams seems to occur to escape danger, as in the following dream.

★ ★ ★

THE FIELD

I'm in a field near the town of Coeyman's Hollow in upstate New York, where I lived for a short time after college. It's one of those glorious spring days when everything is in bloom, the air is cool. Bees are buzzing, birds are singing. A kind of bliss sweeps over me and I fall back into the grass and gaze up into the cerulean blue of the sky.

Suddenly, the ground beneath me begins to tremble, then to shake, as if an earthquake is in progress. I don't think about it, I just react. I leap up so fast I'm airborne.

I flap my arms and sail across the field, 40 or 50 feet above it, and watch as the field breaks apart. As trees topple and a farmhouse caves in, I fly away.

★ ★ ★

If you've never flown in your dreams, you can certainly learn how. People who fly regularly in their dreams report it as one of their most pleasurable dream activities. Flying in your dreams can help you overcome the fear of flying in your waking life. It can also release you from waking tensions, empower you, and completely revamp your ideas of what is possible.

In *The Dream Workbook,* Jill Morris offers an excellent method for learning to fly in your dreams. She suggests that before you go to sleep, think about flying. Visualize what it would be like. As with any visualization, add as many details as you can—the feel of the wind through your hair, how the world would look from a vantage point 50 feet up, how your body would feel. Tell yourself you're going to fly in your dreams, repeat your intention out loud, and repeat it silently to yourself as you begin to drift off. If you wake up during the night, remind yourself of what you want to do.

If you don't succeed the first night, keep at it. In *Creative Dreaming,* Patricia Garfield talks about the dream-flying experiences of Mary Arnold-Foster, "one of the most successful modern inducers of dreams." Arnold-Foster induced flying dreams by repeating her intent to fly throughout the day, as a way of reinforcing her desire to her unconscious mind.

Once the flying dreams began to occur, she was able to increase their frequency by giving herself a specific goal to accomplish in the dream. Arnold-Foster

Exercise 16: A FLYING DREAM EXPERIMENT

Using Jill Morris's technique, write out what you would like to experience in a flying dream. Keep it simple, for example, "I want to fly around my bedroom" or "I want to fly into my back yard." Visualize the experience as you're falling asleep and repeat your written statement several times.

When you wake up, record the results. If you're not successful—and you'll probably know as soon as you're conscious—then shut your eyes and try again. Sometimes, in that lazy state just after waking, it's easy to slip back into a dreaming state.

Write a simple statement about what you would like to accomplish in a flying dream.

Record the results.

Date: Time:

The Dream:

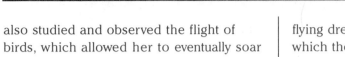

also studied and observed the flight of birds, which allowed her to eventually soar as they did.

"Concentrate on the objects you wish to produce in dreams while you are awake," Garfield advises.

Sometimes in a flying dream, you won't be able to sustain height or even the flight itself. To overcome this, according to Arnold-Foster, you need to have confidence in yourself and not be afraid.

Once you find that flight is possible in a dream, play around with your techniques; be innovative. Try different types of flight. Fly very low to the ground, for instance, as if gliding along like a bee, and then suddenly soar into the sky. If you always take off like Superman, then attempt to fly by standing in one place and flapping your arms.

Some dreamers start out in a small plane, then bail out and "fly on their own"; others find it easier to leap off rooftops or hillsides. One woman, for instance, found that her flying dreams usually began on the roof of her neighbor's house. Initially, she couldn't lift off the rooftop and into the sky; she could only fly to the ground. So she trained herself in her dreams to fly to the next rooftop, and then the next and the next, until one night she ran out of rooftops and there was nowhere to go but up.

According to Stephen LaBerge, in *Exploring the World of Lucid Dreaming,*

flying dreams and lucid dreams (dreams in which the dreamer is conscious) are related. He suggests that when you're not sure if you're dreaming, try to fly. "The easiest way to do this is to hop into the air and attempt to prolong your time off the ground. If you stay airborne for even a split second longer than normal, you can be sure you're dreaming."

Jane Roberts experienced numerous OBEs in her lifetime. During the writing of *The Seth Material,* she decided to see what she could find out about a couple she and her husband knew, who were traveling in Puerto Rico. She laid down, shut her eyes, and gave herself the suggestion that she would find the couple.

Suddenly, she was descending through the air and landed on a porch surrounded by a low railing. "I knew that my body was in bed, but lost all contact with it. Regardless of where it [her body] was, I was someplace else entirely." She took in as many details as she could of her surroundings, and then heard her alarm ringing. Her consciousness snapped back into her body. She wanted more information, so she shut her eyes again and told herself she would return to the same location.

"Brief but definite traveling sensations followed. Mountains and skies swept by. Then I found myself hovering in the air above the same motel." The details she gathered were later verified by her friends.

Near-Death and Out-of-Body Experiences

Near-death experiences (NDEs) are also related to out-of-body travel. The following story, about a woman who had two such near-death experiences, reveals how the phenomenon can lead to very similar experiences in the dream state.

In the early 1960s, a young artist and psychic named Renie had a near-death experience during childbirth. She remembered passing out and then finding herself in the nursery, looking for her daughter, who she knew had been born. She read her daughter's name tag, counted her fingers and toes to make sure they were all there. Then, suddenly, she found herself in "a beautiful place."

"It had gardens, trees, flowers, birds, colors, all the things in nature I love. You couldn't paint a place prettier than this. There were people around—no one I knew, but I wasn't afraid. We started talking. They told me I had to go back and give a message to the doctor who delivered my daughter. That the message was important."

Renie, however, wanted to stay, but was told she had to go back. "The next thing I knew, I was awake, and someone was slapping my face. I was in terrible pain. I grabbed someone's hand and tried to tell the person what had happened. I told the

doctor that I had a message for him, but he didn't want to hear it. He told someone to take me into ICU."

An orderly took her into ICU (intensive care unit). He chatted with her, trying to calm her down, assuring her that the doctor she was trying to talk to didn't listen to anyone. By the time she was settled in her room, she'd forgotten the message.

"Four months or so later, I heard the doctor was shipped out to Vietnam. He never came back. I'm sure that the message I was supposed to give him had to do with that, with Vietnam, that he should get his affairs in order."

Her second NDE occurred in 1968, when Renie died—or so it appeared—of pyla nephritis, a total urinary shutdown. She was about to undergo a biopsy in a North Miami Beach hospital when suddenly the pain and fever disappeared.

"I found myself hovering in a corner of the room, up near the ceiling, watching the doctors trying to resuscitate me. I couldn't understand why it wasn't like it is in the movies, with people shouting codes and a team of people pouring into the room. Once they resuscitated me, I told the main doctor everything that had happened and been said in the room, while they were trying to bring me back."

The near-death research of pioneers such as Dr. Elizabeth Kubler-Ross and Dr. Raymond Moody cleared the way for other near-death survivors to come forward with their own stories. Best-selling books like

UNICORN

To dream of a unicorn, that beautiful creature of ancient mythology, means good fortune and happy circumstances will soon be yours.

A good dream to have, there are many stories about unicorns that have been handed down from generation to generation among people of all countries. However, no one has actually seen a unicorn. Unicorns only exist in dreams!

Embraced by the Light by Betty Eadie indicate there is a profound hunger in Western culture for this kind of material. But back in the early 1960s, when Renie had her first near-death experience, there was no name for the experience. You didn't talk about it.

Renie, however, seized on her experience and began to explore it. She found that she could leave her body with relative ease, sometimes by using a flying dream as a kind of launch pad, other times by simply willing herself "up and out."

By 1981, she knew her way around this inner realm that Monroe charted. On Halloween of that year, she met and fell in love with Mark, a much younger man who had Hodgkin's disease. They were nearly inseparable until his death the following May. A couple of months after he'd died, Renie lay in bed one night, drifting in a half-sleep, thinking about the young man.

"And suddenly I wasn't in bed anymore. Telephone poles were flying past me. And then I was at this convalescent home, being greeted by this woman in a nurse's uniform. She said she would take me to see Mark, but it would have to be a short visit. She took me to his room. He was wearing a dressing gown, and was still confused about the circumstances surrounding his death. He'd been given so many drugs, it was taking time to clear out his etheric body."

Renie explained the circumstances about his death, answered his questions, then the nurse told her she had to leave. "The next thing I knew, I was back in my bedroom, wide awake."

When she dreamed of him again, she saw him on a speedboat, racing across ocean waves. "He looked great, he'd recovered from his death."

Out-of-Body Travel

This section explores how to travel out-of-body while you're asleep.

Robert Monroe's technique, gleaned from his more than thirty years of exploration, is not simple, by any means. However, it is certainly within the reach of anyone committed to dream work.

1. *Relaxation.* There are numerous books available on how to achieve the total relaxation necessary for an OBE. Use whatever method feels right to you. The goal is to reach that drowsy state between wakefulness and sleep and to maintain it without falling asleep.

   "As you become relaxed and start to drift into sleep," Monroe writes, "hold your mental attention on something, anything, with your eyes closed. Once you can hold the borderland state indefinitely without falling asleep, you have passed the first stage."

   The second stage of relaxation is to maintain the borderland state without concentrating on anything. Just focus on the blackness in front of you. Eliminate any nervousness or unease you might feel.

The third stage involves a deepening of consciousness by "letting go of your rigid hold on the borderland sleep edge and drifting deeper little by little . . ." Monroe says that sensory mechanisms begin to shut down. Touch usually goes first, and then smell and taste. Sometimes your vision goes next, sometimes your hearing.

2. *Vibrations.* This is the critical phase. According to Monroe, the vibrational field that is essential to an OBE seems to work best when your head is positioned at magnetic north. Also, make sure your room isn't completely dark; you need some light as a point of reference. In addition, don't set a time limit; and make sure you won't be disturbed.

Without weakening your conscious awareness, relax as deeply as you can, then give yourself the suggestion that you'll recall everything you experience that is beneficial to your "physical and mental being." Monroe suggests that you repeat this five times, then begin breathing with your mouth half opened.

To set up the vibrational waves, he recommends that you imagine two lines extending from the sides of your head and converging about a foot away in front of your eyes. Think of these lines as charged wires that are joined, or as poles of a magnet that are connected. Once they converge, extend them three

feet from your forehead, and then six feet. Now you must move the intersected lines ninety degrees so they meet over your head. Then reach out toward the point through the top of your head. Keep reaching until you feel a reaction. "It is as if a surging, hissing rhythmically pulsating wave of fiery sparks comes roaring into your head," he writes. "From there it seems to sweep throughout your body, making it rigid and immobile."

3. *Controlling the vibrations.* Monroe stresses that eliminating fear and panic is of utmost importance. The first time the vibrations occur, you'll feel like you're being electrocuted, even though there's no pain involved. "Lie quietly and

Exercise 17: MY OUT-OF-BODY EXPERIENCE

Your Technique: Write down the steps you intend to take to induce an OBE. This might be Monroe's method, one of the others, a combination, or your own invention. Whatever steps you decide upon should feel right; they should "click." Include your target area (your bedroom, a friend's house), the date and approximate time, and the results.

Date: ....

Time: ....

Preparation: ....

....

....

....

Relaxation technique: ....

....

....

....

OBE method: ....

....

....

....

Target: ....

....

....

Results: ....

....

....

....

objectively analyze them until they fade away of their own accord. This usually takes place in about five minutes."

Once you become accustomed to the sensation, you're ready to control it. Monroe suggests that you mentally direct the vibrations into a ring that sweeps around your body, from head to toes and back again. Once you've got the momentum going, let it proceed on its own.

It takes practice to smooth out the vibrations. But once you're able to do it, you should be able to start the vibrations simply on a mental command, thus eliminating some of the other steps. The momentum of the vibration is critical to disassociation from the physical. The faster the vibration, the easier it is to disassociate.

4. *Thought control.* Monroe contends that in the out-of-body state, thought is instantaneously translated into action. Because of this, you have to be focused on a single thought, such as "float upward." This is also why you have to eliminate fear and panic. If you don't, your fear will instantly manifest. It might assume some terrifying shape, or it might propel you right back into your body. Fear, Monroe says, is the biggest obstacle to overcome.

5. *Separation and lifting out.* Monroe recommends that you initially separate just your hand and explore the area in the immediate vicinity. Find an object, identify it, and then wake up and see if

you're right. This is a way to build self-confidence.

Once you're comfortable with this partially dissociated state, the easiest way to fully separate from your body is to "lift out." Imagine yourself floating upward. Think about how pleasurable the sensation will be. Imagine yourself getting lighter and lighter. If you hold these thoughts, you'll float upward. You can also rotate your way out—turn over—just as you would if you were trying to get more comfortable in bed. "Start turning by twisting the top of your body, your head and shoulders . . . move slowly . . ."

Once you begin this exploration and can summon the vibrational state at will, "you will be committed to the reality of this other existence. How this will affect your personality, your daily life, your future and your philosophies rests entirely with you as an individual."

Renie's Method

Renie's technique, though simpler than Monroe's, involves the same basics.

1. *Relaxation.* Renie suggests that you enter a relaxed state using whatever method works best for you. Then, when your entire body is relaxed, visualize the OBE happening. See it clearly in your mind, and hold the image.

2. *Visualization.* Once you're completely relaxed and are focused on leaving your body, visualize yourself shrinking. "For me,

this is crucial to getting out. I see myself getting smaller and smaller, until I'm nearly non-existent. If you can't envision this at first, keep practicing until you can."

3. *Vibrational field.* At some point during the shrinking process, a humming may begin in your ears. The humming is comparable to the vibrational field described by Monroe. Remain focused on how small you are and turn up the volume on the humming.

4. *Getting out.* "When I can't possibly shrink anymore without vanishing and when the humming is very loud, I visualize my astral self floating away from my physical body and say, 'Up and out.' And I'm gone."

5. *Thought control.* To travel in the out-of-body state, simply think about where you want to go. The clearer your request, the faster you move—and with fewer impediments.

Tholey's Method

Yet another method of achieving the out-of-body state is offered by Paul Tholey, a German psychologist who has researched OBEs and lucid dreams. He calls his method "body technique." Tholey recommends that, while drifting into sleep, you imagine that your body is somewhere else, doing something other than lying in bed. If

you find yourself "elsewhere," you have achieved the OBE state.

Alternately, Tholey suggests concentrating on the idea that as you are falling asleep you will no longer perceive your body. Then, as soon as you are asleep, it is possible to float freely, at a point of awareness, in "a space which seems to be identical with the room in which one went to sleep."

Other Hints

Keep in mind that when you travel out of body, there are no guarantees that your experience will be pleasant. The worlds you will visit are not necessarily any better or worse than the physical one in which you exist. But if you do find yourself in a "lower realm" among disturbed beings, there are ways of effectively dealing with them, and moving on. When Jane Roberts encountered undesirable people, or "energy shapes," on her early out-of-body travels, Seth advised her not to panic. If the entity seemed threatening, she was supposed to say, "Peace be with you," and this would dissipate the negative emotion that fueled the entity.

Pay special attention to your ordinary dreams during this time. If your anxieties and fears are emerging in the dreams, work through whatever caused them. Knowing what you fear is the first step in conquering the fear itself. Once you've conquered the fears, your OBEs will progress more smoothly.

CHAPTER THIRTEEN

Lucid
Dreaming

A lucid dream is one in which you're aware that you're dreaming. It may begin as a normal dream, but at some point you "wake up" inside the dream. Then, depending on your skill, you manipulate the action in the dream, to mold it—to create it second by second.

For years, lucid dreaming was primarily the domain of parapsychologists, a critical factor in discouraging mainstream scientists from studying it. But in recent years, there has been an explosive interest in lucid dreaming. Stephen LaBerge, a pioneer of lucid dreaming research, attributes this surge of interest, in part, to several landmark books.

In 1968, an English parapsychologist named Celia Green published *Lucid Dreams.* Her book contained the most comprehensive overview of the literature available on the subject up to that time.

During the 1970s, Ann Faraday, author of *The Dream Game,* and Patricia Garfield, author of *Creative Dreaming,* were instrumental in kindling popular interest in the subject. Even though serious scientific research of lucid dreaming didn't take place until the 1970s, it has been recognized for

Was it a vision or a waking dream?

—JOHN KEATS

centuries. A Tibetan yoga master wrote about methods of learning the dream skill in an eighth century tome called *The Yoga of the Dream State.* A couple of centuries later, another Tibetan master, Atisha, wrote of being simultaneously awake and asleep in *The Seven Points of Mind Training.*

Earlier this century, the Russian philosopher P.D. Ouspensky asked himself, "Was it not possible to preserve consciousness in dreams, that is, to know while dreaming that one is asleep and to think consciously as we think when awake?" Ouspensky decided the answer was yes. In *A New Model of the Universe,* he recalled the following lucid dream, which he referred to as a half-dream state.

★ ★ ★

I remember once seeing myself in a large empty room without windows. Besides myself there was in the room only a small black kitten. "I am dreaming," I say to myself. "How can I know whether I am really asleep or not? Suppose I try this way. Let this black kitten be transformed into a large white dog. In a waking state it is impossible and if it comes off it will mean that I am asleep." I say this to myself and

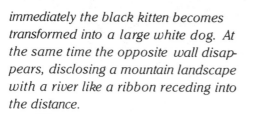

immediately the black kitten becomes transformed into a large white dog. At the same time the opposite wall disappears, disclosing a mountain landscape with a river like a ribbon receding into the distance.

"This is curious," I say to myself; "I did not order this landscape. Where did it come from?" Some faint recollection begins to stir in me, a recollection of having seen this landscape somewhere and of its being somehow connected with the white dog. But I feel that if I let myself go into it I shall forget the most important thing that I have to remember, namely, that I am asleep and am conscious of myself . . .

★ ★ ★

Then, of course, there is Carlos Castaneda. Like Jane Roberts, his work began in the early 1960s. In his first book, *The Teachings of Don Juan,* Castaneda recounts his apprenticeship with a Yaqui Indian sorcerer named don Juan.

There has been considerable controversy about whether Castaneda's books are colorful fiction or fictionalized versions of true events. Regardless, the fact remains that the dream states Castaneda writes about, in which he explores different worlds, very similar to lucid dreaming. One of the "cues" don Juan taught Castaneda for becoming conscious in a dream is worth mentioning here. In *Journey to Ixtlan,* don Juan shows him how to find

his hand in a dream as a way of stabilizing the dream. We now know that this might be useful as a clue that you are lucid.

For one man, a science fiction writer, seeing his hand in a dream didn't prove to be just "useful." It saved his life.

★ ★ ★

JAY'S HAND

My wife and I had a beef dinner that night. I don't remember feeling unusual in any way. We went to bed early and at some point during the night, I dreamed that I saw my hand. That was it, just my hand. I could see it clearly.

And suddenly I realized I was dreaming and I snapped awake. I could hardly breathe. My chest felt heavy, I thought I was having a heart attack. I woke my wife and she called the paramedics.

Since we lived on a farm then, out in the middle of nowhere, it took them a long time to arrive. My wife and my closest friend, who was staying over that night, kept me alive until the paramedics got there.

The upshot was that I'm allergic to red meat and the beef I'd eaten that night caused an adrenaline reaction. If I hadn't dreamed of seeing my hand, I might not have awakened in time to save my life.

★ ★ ★

In the following example, the dreamer was a young woman who had been involved in lucid dreaming work.

THE CLOCK

In the dream, my alarm hadn't gone off and I knew I would be late for work. I was running around, trying to eat and shower and get dressed, all in the space of a few minutes.

At some point, it occurred to me that I didn't really have any idea what time it was and that's when the dream became lucid, when I woke inside the dream. I suddenly realized that if I turned my head ever so slightly, I would be able to see my clock on the night-stand. So that's what I did. The time was 3:07.

I opened my eyes, coming fully awake, and the clock read 3:07.

LaBerge himself didn't realize that lucid dreaming was possible until the fall of 1976, when he ran across Celia Green's book: ". . . if others had learned to have lucid dreams, then nothing prevented me from doing the same. Just reading about the topic had resulted in several lucid dreams for me." In February of 1977, he began a dream journal and over the next seven years, he recorded nearly nine hundred lucid dreams.

LaBerge used lucid dreaming as the basis for his doctoral thesis, then procured space at the Stanford University Sleep Research Center where he could conduct his experiments.

At the time, mainstream science still believed that lucid dreaming was impossible. So when LaBerge submitted his preliminary findings to the prestigious magazine *Science,* the paper was rejected. The British magazine equivalent, *Nature,* returned his paper unreviewed; their editors didn't think the topic of lucid dreaming was "of sufficient interest" to even merit consideration.

Despite the resistance by mainstream science, LaBerge persevered and by the mid-80s, the scientific climate toward lucid dreams had begun to change. By then, he was well into his exploration and was working regularly with "oneironauts"—a word he coined from Greek roots—or "explorers of the inner world of dreams." He had taught these oneironauts how to signal when a lucid dream began. He developed certain criteria and techniques for inducing and exploring lucid dreams and believes that anyone can learn them.

Your First Lucid Dream

Frequently, lucid dreams are first experienced "accidentally." In other words, no special preparations are made, but a dream sud-

denly turns lucid. You realize you are awake and still dreaming. If you're lucky, the experience will last more than a few seconds.

For some, lucidity may arise for the first time from a nightmare. But for most dreamers, LaBerge says, lucidity happens when you recognize some glaring inconsistency or bizarre factor in your dream. Other times, a first-time experience is triggered when you realize your dream is very familiar, that you've dreamed it before. LaBerge calls this entry into a lucid dream *deja reve*.

In the following example, Anita's recurring dream about a Gothic house triggered a lucid dream.

GOTHIC HOUSE AS LAUNCHPAD

As soon as I stepped into the house this time, I recognized it. I knew it was the Gothic house of my recurring dream, the place I had explored countless times in the past.

With this realization, the dream turned lucid. I found myself in a sunlit living room, an immense and beautifully furnished room that I hadn't been in before. Just to make sure I was actually lucid, I leaped into the air to see if I could fly and I did! My astonishment was so great, I woke up.

The woman's "reality testing" is a reasoning process normally delegated to the waking brain and is one of the elements that distinguishes lucid dreams from other kinds of dreams. With practice, you won't even have to ask if you're dreaming. Once you recognize some anomaly or bizarre event in the dream, your realization will be instantaneous.

If you have never awakened inside a dream and would like to sample the experience, or if you've spontaneously entered a lucid dream in the past and would like to further explore this region of dreaming, there are methods you can try to induce lucidity. The best time to enter a lucid dream is either just as you fall asleep or as you awaken after a night's sleep. If you fall asleep easily and quickly, with practice you can enter a lucid dream within minutes of lying down. LaBerge suggests using a counting method: *One, I'm dreaming; two, I'm dreaming . . .* "The result is that at some point—say, 'forty-eight, I'm dreaming'—you are dreaming!"

Alternately, as you are falling asleep, focus on one particular thing—a visualization, your breath or heartbeat, how your body feels, or whatever you choose. "If you keep the mind sufficiently active while the tendency to enter REM sleep is strong," writes LaBerge, "you feel your body fall asleep but you, that is to say, your consciousness, remains awake."

Or, you may find that a lucid state is easier to obtain after you've slept awhile. Since your longest period of REM sleep is toward morning, try not to open your eyes when you wake. Lie quietly and let your dream images surround and flow through you. Then turn

MILK, CHEESE, CREAM

To dream of milk portends prosperity and happiness. For a farmer dreaming of milk could mean an abundant harvest. For the traveler it means an important and successful voyage. For women to dream of milk means they will possibly be prosperous.

To see large quantities of milk in your dreams means you will be rich and healthy. To dream of giving milk away suggests you are too generous for your own good and your own fortune. Dreaming of sour milk means you will be upset over a friend's distress.

To dream of cream portends wealth. Dreaming of drinking cream—does anyone do that anymore?—means good fortune.

Dreaming of cheese, however, generally means sorrow ahead. Swiss cheese in a dream, on the other hand, means you will come into substantial possessions and have good health.

Exercise 18: MEMORY TRAINING

You may want to train your waking memory for a week by giving yourself four specific targets each day. Memorize the day's targets. Record your successes below. Every time you find one of the targets, write it down, and remember to ask yourself if you're dreaming. Keep track of how many targets you hit each day. If, at the end of the week, you've missed most of the targets, then continue the exercise for another week.

DAY ONE

Targets: ....
....
....
....

Notes: ....
....
....

Hits: ....
....
....

DAY TWO

Targets: ....
....
....
....

Notes: ....
....
....

Hits: ....
....
....

DAY THREE

Targets:

Notes:

Hits:

DAY FOUR

Targets:

Notes:

Hits:

DAY FIVE

Targets:

EXERCISE

DAY FIVE Continued

Notes: ....

....

....

....

Hits: ....

....

....

DAY SIX

Targets: ....

....

....

Notes: ....

....

....

Hits: ....

....

....

DAY SEVEN

Targets: ....

....

....

Notes: ....

....

....

Hits: ....

....

....

SLEEP PATTERNS

The Seth Material and Jane Roberts's own books offer valuable information on dream states. In *The Nature of Personal Reality,* Seth discusses the value of sleeping in four or six-hour blocks instead of the usual eight-hour block that is customary in Western culture.

By following such a sleep routine, ". . . There are not the great artificial divisions created between the two states of consciousness. The conscious mind is better able to remember and assimilate its dreaming experience, and in the dream the self can use the waking experience more efficiently."

Without ever mentioning the term *lucid dreaming,* he says that by following this particular sleep routine, it becomes obvious that "the individual sense of identity can be retained in the dream state. When you find yourself as alert, responsive, and intellectual in the dream state as you are in waking life, it becomes impossible to operate within the old framework."

It's interesting to note that Robert Monroe followed a sleep routine similar to what Seth describes. He frequently mentions sleeping for "two cycles," a reference to two dream cycles of about four hours. Roberts and her husband also followed Seth's suggestions. They slept for six hours a night, with a half-hour nap in the afternoon, as needed.

This routine is dependent on a flexible work schedule, so that you can nap at some point during the day. If your schedule won't allow it, then try the routine on weekends or vacations, when your time is your own.

From the sleep exercise at the beginning of the book, you may have already determined that you need seven hours of sleep at night. In that case, try a six-hour block of sleep at night and take an hour nap in the afternoon or right before dinner. The results may surprise you.

Exercise 19: MY CHALLENGES AND GOALS

List five fears or limitations that you would like to overcome. Also, list five goals that you would like to achieve in the next three months, six month, and in the next year. Create a game plan for incorporating these challenges and goals into your lucid dreaming program. And then put them into action!

Five fears or limitations I would like to overcome: 1.

2.   3.

4.   5.

My game plan for overcoming them:

Five goals I would like to achieve in the next 3 months: 1.

2.   3.

4.   5.

My game plan for achieving my goals:

Five goals I would like to achieve in the next 6 months: 1.

2.   3.

4.   5.

My game plan for achieving my goals:

Five goals I would like to achieve in the next 12 months: 1.

2.   3.

4.   5.

My game plan for achieving my goals:

My affirmation for this work is:

over on your side or change positions. The act of moving may allow you to think of yourself as awake as well as dreaming.

Intent

Your intention to explore the world of lucid dreaming is vital in triggering such a dream. When LaBerge was just beginning his research, he realized that as he clarified his *intent to remember,* the number of lucid dreams he had increased dramatically. "Lucid dreaming rarely occurs without our intending it, which means having the mental set to recognize when we are dreaming; thus, intention forms a part of any deliberate effort to induce lucid dreams."

Malcolm Godwin, author of *The Lucid Dreamer—A Working Guide for the Traveler Between Worlds,* notes that the method advocated by the tenth century Tibetan master Atisha creates a similar effect: *Think that all phenomena are like dreams.* "For in continually thinking that everything is a dream during

the day, that mind-set begins to appear in your nightly dreams, and suddenly you will start to experience yourself both deeply asleep and yet fully awake at the same moment."

LaBerge suggest that you set memory targets during the day as a way of training your mind to wake up during a dream. In this method, you select objects or even sounds as triggers. For example, if you select two targets, the sound of a dog barking and the sight of a red car, you will note that you've found a target whenever you hear a bark or see the appointed vehicle. Importantly, you should also ask yourself if you are dreaming. Do so, even if you are obviously awake.

LaBerge's MILD Technique

If you're not able to remember to do something when you're awake, you probably won't be able to remember to do it when you're asleep. But if you're successful with your target exercise, you should also be able to use LaBerge's MILD (mneumonic induction of lucid dreaming) technique, which is outlined in his book *Exploring the World of Lucid Dreaming.* There are five basic steps.

1. *Set up dream recall.* Step one involves nothing more than stating your intent to wake up through the night and recall your dreams. Or you can pick one particular dream period, like the last one of

the night, when you're most likely to have lucid dreams.

2. *Recall your dream.* When you wake from a dream, try to recall as many details as possible. Don't tell yourself you'll remember the dream in the morning; chances are the dream will be gone by then. Force yourself to write down the dream in your dream journal.

3. *Focus your intent.* While you're falling back to sleep, focus on your intention to recognize that you're dreaming. Mean what you say. Stay centered on this one thought.

4. *Visualize yourself becoming lucid.* The best way to do this is to see yourself back in the dream from which you've just awakened. But this time recognize that it's a dream. Look for something in the experience that will tip you off that you're dreaming. For example, as you relive the dream, decide that you're going to fly. See yourself doing it, see yourself realizing that you're dreaming, and then continue reliving the dream.

5. *Repeat.* LaBerge recommends repeating steps three and four just to fix your intent in your mind.

Mirror, Mirror on the Wall

Malcolm Godwin offers another method of entering a lucid dream that is a variation on an Eastern technique known as *tratak*. He suggests that before going to sleep you set up a mirror and sit comfortably in front of it for about half an hour. Place a lighted candle nearby so that your face is illuminated well. Stare steadily at your reflected image without blinking (if you find that to be difficult, use eyedrops). The face in the mirror will start changing quite dramatically, like a series of wavering masks. Godwin notes that many practitioners believe these masks are images of our past lives.

As you continue to gaze into the mirror, *intend* to dream that night. Watch the changing faces a while longer, and then ask to see your real face. "Meditators claim that in waking life the image in the mirror disappears altogether," Godwin says. "In lucid dreams prepare to be even more surprised."

No matter what method you use to reach the world of lucid dreams, once you begin your journey, the benefits are enormous:

☆ You can overcome your fears by directly confronting them in your lucid dreams.

☆ You can increase your self-knowledge, which expands your awareness.

☆ By consciously facing danger in your dreams, you develop self-confidence, which spills into your everyday life.

☆ You can solve problems in the dream state that will benefit your waking life.

CHAPTER FOURTEEN

Shamanism
and Dreaming

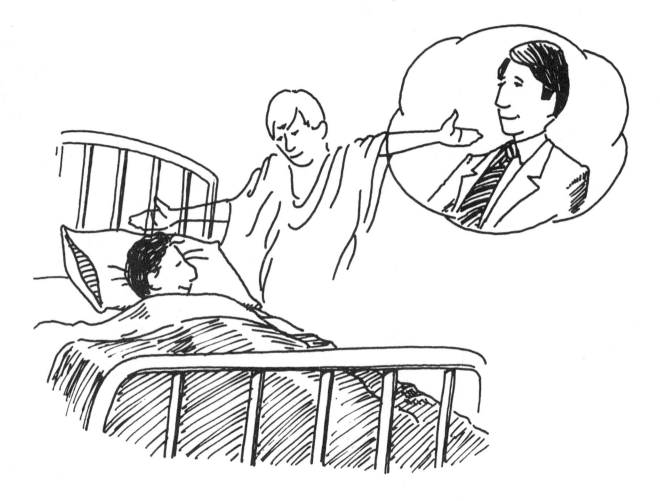

The ancient practice of shamanism is alive today not only in the remnants of primitive cultures but also in a revival by a new age of shamans, many of them raised and educated in the Western world. Most of these Western shamans, no longer called "witch doctors" or "medicine men," have been trained by elders who are part of a primitive culture or who have strong links to one.

> *Dreaming is the bona fide art of breaking the barriers of normal perception.*
>
> — CARLOS CASTANEDA

"Big Dreams"

"A shaman is a man or woman who enters an altered state of consciousness—at will—to contact and utilize an ordinarily hidden reality in order to acquire knowledge, power, and to help other persons," says Michael Harner, an anthropologist who has practiced shamanism for more than a quarter of a century.

Harner says that from the shaman's perspective there are ordinary dreams and "big dreams." The shaman's interest is in the latter. Big dreams involve communication with a guardian spirit or a power animal. "A big dream is one that is repeated several times in the same basic way on different nights, or it is a one-time dream that is so vivid that it is like being awake."

The difference between a shamanic dream, or big dream, and a lucid dream is that the former deals with spirit or guardian contact and/or the intent of gaining power or knowledge. A lucid dream is typically an adventure or journey that is not necessarily connected with any spiritual tradition or related goal.

Harner, director of the Foundation of Shamanic Studies, has held numerous workshops on shamanism, teaching skills that have been handed down over millennia. "In my shamanic workshops, these new practitioners are not 'playing Indian,' but going to the same revelatory spiritual sources that tribal shamans have traveled to from time immemorial. . . . Their experiences are genuine and, when described, are essentially interchangeable with the accounts of shamans from nonliterate tribal cultures."

Big dreams are often literal, and if you dream of being in a car accident, the dream may not be symbolic but a warning of an actual accident. Harner says that in such a case you might not be able to prevent it, but you can enact it symbolically and thereby minimize its impact.

In his book, *The Way of the Shaman*, Harner describes a big dream, recounted by

a woman who had attended one of his workshops. In the dream, she was in a car accident in which she hit metal twice but wasn't seriously injured. Even though she knew about symbolically enacting such a dream, she didn't do it. About a month later, she was driving with her son when a car veered in front of her. She struck the car, was spun around, and struck it again.

"While waiting for the car to stop its 180-degree spin, I was aware of being pinned against my son within the car by the momentum of the spin, and being outside and slightly over the car watching the entire 'dream' taking place—again. During the entire episode I was aware of a feeling of deep peace and the awareness that my guardian spirit was right there with me and shielding me from danger."

Just as in her dream, she struck metal twice and was not seriously injured. She noted that her son was not in her dream, but he received only minor injuries.

Not all big dreams are ominous, Harner says. Some may bode well for the future, showing hints or patterns of what is to come. In those cases, the dream should also be enacted, but this time with the intent to enhance it, rather than diminish its impact.

You don't have to be a shaman or even a shaman's apprentice to enact a "big dream." The technique can be carried out whenever you have a particularly vivid dream, whether it's ominous or providential.

First, ask yourself what the message is, and then decide whether it is literal or symbolic. Either way, you can enact the dream.

The experience of Gary H. is an example of how to do it.

When Gary H. had a brief, but vivid, dream, its contents were so startling that he bolted out of his sleep and sat up gasping for breath. In the dream, he had taken a gun, put it to his head, and fired. Bright red blood spurted from the wound and he knew he had just killed himself.

Gary was puzzled by the dream, because he wasn't suicidal and had never thought about killing himself. However, he had recently left his wife and was starting out on a new life. He realized that the dream image was symbolic of killing his old self. He would never be the same person again.

He enacted the dream by beginning divorce proceedings, even though his wife wanted to wait to see if matters could be patched up. He felt that there was no going back to the old ways and that the dream was a confirmation. It was a difficult, highly emotional situation, but he felt he was taking the right action.

He also made a symbolic gesture to move ahead into his new life by visualizing a frayed rope connecting him and his wife. In the visualization, he took a scissors and cut the remaining threads.

Dreams of Power

"Shamanism is not a religion," explains Alberto Villoldo, a medical anthropologist and an Inca shaman. "There is no Christ figure,

Exercise 20: ENACTING A BIG DREAM

If you have a dream that you consider a big dream, describe it here. Then, plan the way that you will enact the dream and the results.

Date: ....

Dream description: ....

....

....

....

....

....

Enactment plan: ....

....

....

....

....

....

Description of the actual enactment: ....

....

....

....

....

....

Outcome: ....

....

....

....

....

Mortgage, deed, property

To dream of taking a mortgage on property you own means financial upheavals to come that might put you into a difficult position. So don't mortgage the farm. If you dream you own vast property, you will have great success in life.

To dream of signing a deed portends a lawsuit. Select your counsel carefully as you are likely to be a loser. A dream that you sign any paper is a bad omen, even if you are signing receipts of monies given to you—so be careful what you sign in a dream.

FOR SALE

no Buddha, no guru, nobody who says, 'Follow my footsteps.' Shamanism demands that you take your own steps with courage, compassion, and vision. It requires that you learn from nature. It teaches you to meet power directly, embrace it, and claim it."

Villoldo's sojourn into shamanism began in 1973, when he met Antonio Morales Baca, a philosophy professor at the Universidad Nacional de San Antonio Abad in Cuzco and the only Indian on the university's staff. With Morales as a guide, they set out on a trek along the Urubamba River in the altiplano in search of a *kurac akullec,* a master shaman named don Jicaram. Ultimately, Villoldo realized that Morales and don Jicaram were one and the same, and he began his fourteen-year apprenticeship, which is described in his books, *Dance of the Four Winds* and *Island of the Sun.*

In the latter book, Villoldo tells of a waking dream sequence that reveals itself to be dreams within dreams. It began after arriving at Machu Picchu on a solo trek of the Inca Trail. He stole into the ruins as darkness fell and found a secluded alcove. Unable to sleep, he crossed the central plaza under a full moon and moved to a meadow that edged the ruins near the Pachamama Stone, an upright slab 20 feet wide and 10 feet high.

His experience began with a meditation that led to his vision of an ancient Inca ceremony in which several colorfully garbed participants were dancing and chanting around the fire near the Pachamama Stone. He joined the dancers and then followed one of them—a young girl with plaited hair woven with ribbons—away from the fire and along a trail leading up Huayna Picchu, a steep mountain peak near the ruins.

The girl disappeared among the rocks, and he came to a cavern where he met an old woman who seemed to be waiting for him. The woman, who was busy making candles from animal lard, spoke rudely to him.

"My first thought was that I was dreaming; it was a fact that I was dreaming, I was *aware* that I was dreaming. And then the room collapsed . . . and in the dream I see myself, sitting before the Pachamama Stone, and the dancers are moving in the soft rain and the orange light of the fire. I knew that somewhere I was in my body and dreaming about myself watching the dancers down there. . . . That is a dream. And this?"

He found himself back in the cavern with the old woman. He described her in detail, from the bone pipe she was smoking to her woven wool dress, but he couldn't hear what she was saying to him. He followed her out of the cavern and over to a pair of huge condors. Then the old crone taught him how to project himself into an animal. He did so, merging with the consciousness of one of the condors and soaring through the night. When he returned to the cavern, the old woman told him to leave.

He tried to go back to his dream. He knew that he had to be dreaming again to wake himself up. "And when I see myself sleeping in the meadow before the Pachamama Stone, I struggle to wake myself. The dancers have gone and dawn is threatening to break and I am asleep on the grass.

HOW TO OBTAIN A POWER DREAM

To obtain a power dream, you don't necessarily need a shaman to guide you or even a power object from an ancient lineage of shamans. You may have a power object in your own possession without even realizing it.

Such an object might be a family heirloom that has been passed down from generation to generation. Perhaps, a wedding ring that belonged to your grandmother that had once belonged to her mother or grandmother. The idea is that such an object has "stored memories" or messages that can be accessed through shamaniclike dreaming.

To prepare for your power dream, hold the object in your hand before going to bed. Quiet your mind. It's okay if you don't know the history of the object. Note any thoughts that seem to come to your mind from elsewhere after you've quieted your thoughts. If any of them seem to be warnings, heed them and don't go any further. To that end, make sure you don't knowingly select an object that belonged to a mentally disturbed person. The result could be a distressing nightmare.

After your meditation, place the object under your pillow or someplace in close proximity to your body. As you fall asleep, concentrate on your desire to receive a dream of power from someone once associated with the object. Tell yourself that only a positive experience will result and that your life will be enhanced by the dream.

. . . It is only when I see myself stir and watch my eyes open that I realize that I am dreaming of myself waking in the meadow."

It was that dream, of watching himself wake up and inspect the ground where the dancers had trod, from which he truly and fully awoke. He found that he was not in the meadow at all, but in a cavern in the side of Huayna Picchu, a mountain adjacent to Machu Picchu.

Villoldo is now a shaman associated with the Q'ero Indians of the Andes, who are considered direct descendants of the ancient Incas. For more than twenty years, Villoldo has led workshops and shamanic journeys. Rachel, a mother of three, who joined Villoldo on one of his treks to the canyonland of the Southwest, recalls a dream of power that she experienced.

Use the following to record the experience.
Notes

Date:

Power object:

Thoughts about the object before going to sleep:

Results:

Date:

Power object:

Thoughts about the object before going to sleep:

Results:

Date:

Power object:

Thoughts about the object before going to sleep:

Results:

GUITAR, BANJO, HARP

Dreaming of someone playing a banjo portends that pleasant times will soon be enjoyed by you. Whereas if you hear a sweet, sad harp—what seems a pleasing and pleasurable experience in your life is soon going to end.

If you dream of yourself with a guitar, you will soon be part of a fun gathering. If weird music is coming from the guitar, beware and guard against flattery that might tempt you.

And if you are a man who dreams of playing a guitar, you soon will be courted by a crafty, seductive woman! Beware!

★ ★ ★

THE BLACK PANTHER

One evening, Alberto unwrapped his "mesa," a bundle of handwoven cloth, which contained ancient power objects—carved stone figures, metal pieces, bead necklaces, crystals, and cloth bags containing things that rattled. All the power objects had been handed down from Inca shaman to Inca shaman and finally to Villoldo. Some of them were hundreds of years old.

The objects were passed around the circle in the dimly lit tent. Rather than looking at them, we felt them. We were to select one that appealed to us, then quickly pass on the others. That night we were to sleep with the power object we had selected.

My dream began by seeing mountains around me. Somehow, I knew I was in South America. I didn't understand why I was seeing another place, since we were in the Southwest. Then I saw the black panther. It came right into my forehead through a physical opening. Everything opened up then and I had a sense of being in a primordial lost paradise of the Native American. I sensed the people and the earth.

★ ★ ★

Rachel's power object was a small, smooth stone wrapped in a rough piece of cloth. Villoldo told her he wasn't surprised that she'd seen South American mountains and experienced the cat entering her forehead. The stone had been given to him by the high shaman of the Q'eros, the Incan equivalent of the Dalai Lama.

That same night Charles, who was also on the same journey, selected a smooth, three-pronged stone as his power object. "I dreamed of seeing myself dressed and packed for a journey. I was on a train and directly above me was a woman, who was also me. Then there was my dreaming self who was observing the other two.

After relating the dream, Villoldo told him that the three-pronged stone was associated with the three worlds of the Incas: the *Kaypacha,* the physical world; the *Ukhupacha,* the inner world or dreaming world; and *Hanaqpacha,* the higher world. "We all have multiple selves living simultaneously in each of these worlds."

Dream Control

Undoubtedly the most famous practitioner of shamanism, or sorcery, as he calls it, is Carlos Castaneda. His Native American teacher, don Juan, stresses the importance of dream voyages. "Dreams are, if not a door, a hatch into other worlds." According

Exercise 21: CONTROLLING YOUR DREAM

Keep track of your results and add a section in your dream journal for this exercise.

Attempts to see my hands

Date:

Results:

Date:

Results:

Date:

Results:

Attempts to stop the dream

Date:

Results:

Date:

Results:

Date:

Results:

to don Juan, what we call reality is only a description of the world in which we are currently engaged, and that description can be altered through dreaming.

When he began his instruction in dreaming, don Juan taught Castaneda to set up dreams as a means of controlling them. Castaneda explains that the reason to control dreams is to engage your "dreaming atten-

tion," in order to shift your perceptions to new worlds or new ways of seeing this world.

"To set up dreaming means to have a precise and practical command over the general situation of a dream," don Juan says in Castaneda's *The Art of Dreaming*. "For example, you may dream that you are in your classroom. To set up dreaming means that you don't let the dream slip into some-

FINDING YOUR HANDS

The following procedure can help you find your hands during a dream and take control of your dreaming. It's derived from a technique practiced by George Gurdjieff, a nineteenth century Russian mystic teacher.

First, close your eyes and visualize your hands during the day from time to time. Then, as you lie down to sleep, remind yourself of what you've been doing during the day and visualize your hands again. Take this image with you as you fall asleep. Tell yourself that when you see your hands again you will be dreaming, and you will become awake in your dream.

Once you have succeeded in finding your hands, go on to the second part of the procedure: stopping your dream. It may take many attempts before you are able to do this. Before going to sleep, tell yourself that you will find your hands in a dream and then you will be able to stop the dream and carefully examine your surroundings.

After finding your hands in a dream, tell yourself that you are awake and dreaming and in control of the dream. Then freeze the action. Know that you can do it. Look around and examine your surroundings. And remember all that you see.

Keep in mind that it may take weeks or even months before you see your hands, but with practice and consistency, it's likely that you'll succeed. It took Castaneda several months before he saw his hands, and Gurdjieff's disciples reported results in three to six months.

For Gurdjieff, the practice of visualizing hands during the day undermines our ideas about our certainty that we are awake. It was his belief that we're all asleep and that when we finally awaken, we will realize that what we thought of as being awake was actually a dream.

thing else. You don't jump from the classroom to the mountains, for instance. In other words, you control the view of the classroom and don't let it go until you want to."

But to reach that state of control takes practice. The first step for Castaneda was to be able to find his hands in his dreams. To do so helps you become aware that you are dreaming. Once this state of awareness is achieved, you can stop the action within a dream and closely examine your surroundings.

When you can control your dreams as just described, you will have passed through the "first gate" of dreams. "The most astonishing thing that happens to dreamers is that, on reaching the first gate, they also reach the energy body," and the energy body, don Juan says, "can transport itself in one instant to the ends of the universe."

Dreaming the World

The Australian Aborigines, whose shamanic traditions are said to reach back forty thousand years, regard dreaming, or Dreamtime, as the foundation of the world. "Dreams continue to connect the Aboriginal people with what they call Dreamtime, a primal state which embraces the creation of the world at the very dawn of time," writes Malcolm Godwin, in *The Lucid Dreamer*. "Dreamtime is the realm of the mythical beings who first breathed life into the universe."

Another of the new shamans, John Perkins, emphasizes that the dream which created this world is only one version of the world, and that we can create new versions and new worlds. Perkins describes a shaman as "a man or woman who journeys into Dreamtime or parallel worlds and uses the subconscious, along with physical reality, to effect change. . . ."

Perkins first encountered shamans when he worked in the Peace Corps in the Amazon rain forest in the late 1960s. Later, he was trained by indigenous Ecuadorian shamans. Today, he teaches workshops on shamanism and leads groups to the Amazon and the Shuar on ecologically oriented tours.

Dreaming is at the heart of the world of the Shuar, Perkins explains in *The World as You Dream It: Shamanic Teachings from the Amazon and Andes.* In fact, the title of his book summarizes their philosophy that the world is created through our dreams. When he writes of the Shuar's dreaming, Perkins is referring to the collective dream of a people, the dream of how we perceive the world.

"If the world is as we dream it, then every reality is a matter of perception. . . . When we give our energy to a different world, the world is transformed."

But to create a new world, we must first create a new dream.

CHAPTER FIFTEEN

ESP in Dreams

Extra sensory perception (ESP) dreams can be telepathic (involving mind-to-mind communication) or precognitive (involving events in the future). These types of dreams may concern you or your family, friends or acquaintances, strangers or public figures, and private or public events and situations. They are as diverse as the people who dream them.

"ESP dreams," writes Stase Michaels, in *The Bedside Guide to Dreams,* "show us that the psyche is capable of a wide range of psychic dynamics."

Many ESP dreams involve the people who are closest to you, but in the dreams your relationship to the people may be completely different from what they are in waking life. The dreams may be extraordinarily vivid and incredibly colorful, with intense emotional content. Ordinary dreams can also possess these qualities, of course, but with an ESP dream there are distinctive characteristics that stick with you.

Psi researcher Alan Vaughan recalls a dream he had two nights after watching one

> *Dreams are my compass and my truth; they guide me and link me to the divine.*
>
> — JUDITH ORLOFF,
> *SECOND SIGHT*

of his favorite writers, Kurt Vonnegut, Jr., on a television talk show. In the dream, recorded on March 13, 1970, he and Vonnegut were in a house full of children. The novelist was planning to leave on a trip, and then he mentioned that he was moving to an island named Jerome.

Vaughan wrote Vonnegut about the dream and two weeks later received this reply. "Not bad. On the night of your dream, I had dinner with Jerome B., and we talked about a trip I made three days later to an island named England."

Telepathic Dreams about Family Members

In his book *Parent-Child Telepathy,* psychiatrist Berthold Schwartz recorded over five hundred instances of telepathy within his own family. Many of the episodes involved trivial but fascinating incidents from daily life, which led Schwartz to believe that telepathy is the "missing link" in communication between parents and their children.

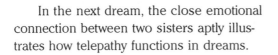

In the next dream, the close emotional connection between two sisters aptly illustrates how telepathy functions in dreams.

★ ★ ★

SISTERS

When my younger sister was a freshman in college, I was in graduate school at the same university. We saw a lot of each other and were close friends during this time.

One Friday night, I dreamed that I was staying at her place off campus, but it looked different than the actual apartment. The hall was long and narrow and the floor buckled in the middle. There were many closed doors off the hallway, and I didn't seem to know which one to open to find whatever I was looking for. I was afraid of opening the wrong one.

I finally stopped in front of a heavy wooden door; I touched the knob. The door wasn't locked, so I pushed it open and stepped inside. It was completely dark and I heard my sister shouting my name; she sounded frightened. I woke with a start and for seconds afterward, her voice seemed to echo in my bedroom. It spooked me.

The next day, I found out that her car had broken down as she and her roommate were on their way back to their place from a party. It had happened about the same time I'd had the dream.

★ ★ ★

The following dream may be a case of telepathy as well as precognition. A woman dreamed of another woman she barely knew. But in the dream the two seemed to know each other well, which soon proved to be the case.

★ ★ ★

TEARDROP

When my daughter was in preschool, she was friendly with a girl whose mother I met and liked. Sue and I agreed to meet for lunch one day, and I decided to squeeze in a nap before I left.

I dreamed that while Sue and I were talking great waves of sadness washed over me; a single teardrop rolled down her cheek. That's all I recall of the dream. But I remember thinking it was a totally bizarre dream because she seemed so vivacious, so full of life and optimism.

When we got together that evening, we talked for a long time, like old friends, and I realized how accurate my dream was. She and her husband were on the verge of divorce. Since then, we've become close friends and see each other more often than our daughters see each other.

★ ★ ★

OAK, WILLOW, PALM TREES

To dream of a mighty oak portends success. Dreaming of a forest of oak trees signifies you will have prosperity in all aspects of your life.

But, dreaming of a willow indicates you will soon make a sad journey and be consoled by your friends.

A dream about palm trees denotes that you are in a hopeful situation and happiness will soon be yours. If a woman dreams of an avenue of palms, she will have a cheerful home and faithful husband.

Exercise 22: MY TELEPATHIC DREAMS

Describe five dreams you've had that involved telepathy. Tell how the dreams demonstrated telepathy and how they differed from ordinary dreams.

Date: .... Time: ....

Dream 1 ....

....

....

....

How this dream demonstrated telepathy: ....

....

....

How this dream differed from an ordinary dream: ....

....

....

★   ★   ★

Date: .... Time: ....

Dream 2 ....

....

....

....

How this dream demonstrated telepathy: ....

....

....

How this dream differed from an ordinary dream: ....

....

....

Date: .... Time: ....

Dream 3 ....

....

....

....

How this dream demonstrated telepathy: ....

....

....

....

How this dream differed from an ordinary dream: ....

....

....

★　　★　　★

Date: .... Time: ....

Dream 4 ....

....

....

....

How this dream demonstrated telepathy: ....

....

....

....

How this dream differed from an ordinary dream: ....

....

....

Additional Comments: ....

....

....

RELIGION, DEVOTION, REVIVAL

If you should dream about religion—particularly the religion in which you were raised—and in your dream you are discussing that religion, it indicates your business affairs will be disagreeable. And also watch out for much adversity.

Dreaming that you are attending a religious revival signifies a family disturbance is about to happen and you will have unprofitable engagements. If

you dream you take part in the revival, you will receive much displeasure from your friends.

If you dream of religious devotion, watch out for deceit in business. But if you are a farmer and dream of being religious and devout, it signifies you will have a good harvest.

If a woman dreams of being religiously devout, it denotes she is chaste and she will have an adoring husband.

Psychiatrist Montague Ullman notes that in his research during the 1960s and 1970s telepathic dreams were more frequently reported by women than by men. However, given the increased public awareness about the value of dreams, this division may no longer be true.

While ESP dream research was once confined to dream laboratories and conducted by scientists, it has spread into dream groups, where participants may be bound together only by their interest in dreams. In many of these groups, no professional dream researchers are involved.

Dream experiments in telepathy have even been conducted among strangers communicating through on-line services. In one such experiment, called The Dream Game, the group was divided into a sender, receivers, and an observer. The sender was responsible for selecting an object and visualizing it going out to the receivers. The sender also provided the observer with a description of the object—it's shape, color, texture, history, location, and other pertinent details. The receivers related the resulting dreams to the sender and observer.

Gary Joy, who started the game on Prodigy, recalled that the first time he played he sent out an image of his dog, Skip, who had recently been put to sleep. None of the people involved knew about the dog or its death. "Out of the ten people, nine had dreams of being separated from something or someone they loved. And, eight of the dreams were about an animal that had died."

The importance of such nonscientific experiments is the recognition that we are all explorers of the dreamscape. The anecdotal information we glean from these explorations is as important, on a personal level, as anything proven in a lab.

The Inner Senses

In the course of a lifetime, you may recall a single telepathic or precognitive dream or you may recall hundreds. It depends on how actively you explore your personal dreamscapes and how deeply you penetrate the layers of yourself.

"When you look into yourself, the very effort involved extends the limitations of your consciousness, expands it, and allows the egotistical self to use abilities that it often does not realize it possesses," says Seth in *The Seth Material*.

He calls these abilities the "inner senses." They often manifest in nonordinary dreams, about public situations. In the following example, a woman named Jan dreamed about the collapse of a major airline more than a decade before it happened.

Exercise 23: MY PRECOGNITIVE DREAMS

Describe four precognitive dreams you've had. Did they involve world events? Something in your personal life? Provide as much detail as you can. Describe how these dreams differed from telepathic dreams. What characteristics made them unique?

Date: .... Time: ....

Dream 1: ....

....

....

....

How this dream demonstrated precognition: ....

....

....

How this dream differed from an ordinary dream: ....

....

....

★   ★   ★

Date: .... Time: ....

Dream2: ....

....

....

....

How this dream demonstrated precognition: ....

....

....

How this dream differed from an ordinary dream: ....

....

....

Date: .... Time: ....

Dream3: ....

....
....
....

How this dream demonstrated precognition: ....

....
....

How this dream differed from an ordinary dream: ....

....
....

★   ★   ★

Date: .... Time: ....

Dream4: ....

....
....
....

How this dream demonstrated precognition: ....

....
....

How this dream differed from an ordinary dream: ....

....
....

Additional Comments: ....

....
....

★ ★ ★

EASTERN AIRLINES

I'm hurrying through a crowded airport, making my way to the Eastern counter with my ticket. When I get there, the counter is deserted. Panicked, I run over to the information booth to find out what's going on. The woman behind the booth, a prissy type with horn-rim glasses, looks at me like I've just asked a ridiculous question.

"They've gone under," she says.

"Under? What do you mean by under?"

"They declared bankruptcy, then disbanded. It was in all the papers."

She then whips out a newspaper and shows me the lead story on Eastern's collapse. I try to read the date, but it's too blurred. I had this dream in late 1974.

★ ★ ★

Jan was able to access an inner sense that has to do with time. "According to Seth," writes Jane Roberts, "these Inner Senses are used by the whole self constantly. Since past, present, and future have no basic reality, this (particular) sense allows us to see through the apparent time barriers. We are seeing things as they really are. Any precognitive experience would entail use of this Inner Sense."

As many researchers emphasize, you don't have to be a prophet to have prophetic dreams. They happen all the time to ordinary people.

Even though Jan's dream happened years before Eastern's demise, it doesn't mean that the future is predetermined. The dream depicted one possible version of the future, based on the patterns that were prevalent at that time for the airline. In this sense, precognitive dreams seem to operate on the same principle as divination.

In 1865, Abraham Lincoln dreamed that he heard strange sounds coming from the East Room of the White House. When he investigated, he saw a corpse resting on a "catafalque," a funeral platform. He saw soldiers standing around the body, guarding it, while a throng of people stared at it. The face was covered, so Lincoln asked one of the guards who had died. "The president," the guard replied.

A week later, Lincoln was assassinated.

Careers have been built on such predictions. One such prophecy was reported in the May 13, 1956, issue of *Parade* magazine. "As for the 1960 election, Mrs. (Jeane) Dixon thinks it will be dominated by labor and won by a Democrat. But he will be assassinated or die in office, though not necessarily in his first term."

Jeane Dixon was, of course, talking about John Kennedy. Even though Dixon was wrong about other things, this prediction tended to stick in people's minds.

History's most famous prophet is Nostradamus. He used nothing more than a

FRUIT, APPLES, PEARS, PLUMS

A dream about apples generally is a good dream. Red apples on a green-leafed tree means good news is coming your way. And dreaming of ripe apples means it's time for you to realize your dreams and hopes. If the apples are ripe on top of the tree, don't aim too high. If the apples are on the ground, watch out for false friends. If you should dream of decayed apples, it signifies that your efforts in your financial endeavors are hopeless.

Dreaming of pears, however, does not always mean a future of success. Dreaming of eating pears portends poor success and ill health. If you are admiring pears on a tree, the future looks promising—more promising than it did previously.

If you dream of ripe plums, you will have a joyous occasion to attend. If you dream of eating plums, expect a flirtatious affair. If you are gathering plums in your dream, it signifies that you will obtain all your desires.

bowl of water to focus his prodigious abilities. By focusing on the water, he was able to enter a dreamlike state in which visions appeared to him.

His reputation as a seer was already established by the time he predicted the death of King Henry II in a jousting tournament. Depending on which interpretation of his writings you read, he also correctly predicted the death of John Kennedy, the fall of the Berlin Wall and of Communism, the alliance between the Soviets and the Americans, the AIDS plague, and the explosion of the Challenger.

Nostradamus, like Edgar Cayce and other psychics, also predicted a pole shift, in which the Earth would tilt on its axis, hurling the planet into utter chaos and destruction. Nostradamus even gave a date—May 5, 2000. Cayce didn't give a specific date, but he did predict geological changes of massive magnitude.

He said that the western part of North America would break up, with California falling into the sea as a result of "the big one." Florida would become a series of islands and "the greater portion of Japan must go into the sea."

If, however, the future is malleable, and if, as some philosophies claim, the consciousness of the planet is connected with the consciousness of man, then this millennium catastrophe can be mitigated or avoided if human beings take

responsibility for their actions. But change on a global scale can only be achieved by change within individuals on a massive scale. Part of this change, according to Seth, takes place in the dream state.

Rose, a nurse, dreamed the next two dreams, but about fifteen years apart. In the first dream, the global situation impacts her life directly; in the second dream, it impacts the life of her daughter. The basic theme is the same.

★ ★ ★

THE BAHAMAS

I'm panicky. Water is everywhere. It's flooding my backyard and is beginning to seep into my living room. It's raining very hard outside, but I understand the flood isn't caused by just the rains, it has something to do with the rising oceans.

In the next scene, I'm running around outside, sloshing through all this water, trying to find a rowboat that I can take to the Bahamas. I know the Bahamas are safe, that the land is rising there. I apparently find a rowboat, because in the final scene I'm headed through a raging sea toward the Bahamas.

I bolt out of this dream so fast I nearly roll out of bed.

★ ★ ★

THE NIGHT AFTER

The night after my daughter was born, I was in a ward with three other women. It was late, nearly two o'clock in the morning, and the nurse had just left with my daughter, after her feeding. I was falling asleep and heard someone call my name. I thought it was one of the women in the ward and snapped upright, but everyone was asleep.

I remember that the door was cracked open, so light seeped into the ward from the hall. I could hear a phone ring and the soft hiss of the cool air coming through the ceiling vents. I laid back down and fell asleep again.

I heard my name called a second time, a loud, piercing shout, and realized it was an internal voice. So I kept my eyes shut, not entirely sure whether I was dreaming or not, and opened myself to the experience.

I had a painfully clear mental image of my daughter—who was absolutely beautiful—about thirty years in the future. She was intent on her task. I understood that she was in the midst of a hypnotic regression or its equivalent and tried to communicate my willingness to cooperate in whatever she was trying to find out.

Mentally, she asked me to verify her birth data. Where were we living when she was born? What time was she born? What hospital? Questions like that.

During the exchange, I had the distinct impression that I was no longer alive. I felt she was speaking to me from a future in which the world was vastly different. The world as I knew it no longer existed. Massive geological changes had happened.

I sensed that pockets of humanity had survived and these people were struggling to come to terms with what had happened. They possessed knowledge about the true nature of time and space. They were capable, in some sense, of manipulating time and space. I'm not sure what that means.

At any rate, I gave her the information she requested and told her that I loved her. She thanked me, and the dream or experience or whatever it was ended.

★ ★ ★

Rose's take on her two dreams is that the futures predicted by Nostradamus and Cayce are two distinct possibilities. But the Earth changes seem to happen at a later date than predicted.

"In the first dream, which I had in the early seventies, my sense was that the destruction would occur within the next ten or fifteen years, sometime during the early or late 1980s. In the second dream, which I had on September 1, 1989, the destruction seemed more distant. Since my daughter was about thirty, that would put her in the

year 2019 or thereabouts and she was already living in this profoundly changed world. It's as if these two dreams depicted two different timelines, two different probabilities, linked because both involved geologically changed worlds."

Although Rose thinks the dreams represent a pattern for the future, she believes what she saw is only one possibility. "I have to believe that the future is not written in stone, that it's possible to avoid some of the catastrophes, at least the man-made ones."

As you become more proficient at interpreting your dreams, telepathic and precognitive dreams will be easier to spot. You may want to keep these kinds of dreams in a special section in your journal or mark them in some way. These dreams are your most intimate link to your own future.

CHAPTER SIXTEEN

Past Lives and Dreams

About two-thirds of the world's population believe that the soul or some other aspect of the human personality not only survives but is reborn time and again. Reincarnation is intrinsic to Eastern religions; and it is also found among Shiite Moslems and certain African tribal groups. In the Western world, the interest in past lives is often associated with New Age concepts.

Although there is nothing new about reincarnation, the interest in exploring past lives through hypnotic regression and through dreams is opening new doors for more and more spiritual adventurers.

"Perhaps the ninety percent of the brain that is rarely put to use holds memories not only of what's happening now, but of what happened in the past—the past of past lifetimes," explains Stase Michaels, author of *The Bedside Guide to Dreams.* "And because dreams draw images from your unconscious, it would not be surprising if every now and then a dream accidentally touched a vivid memory from a past life and replayed it for you, just like the discovery of old photographs in an attic . . ."

> *Not all dreams are Freudian dreams with symbols, distortions, and wish—metaphors. Some dreams convey literal past life memories.*
>
> —BRIAN WEISS,
> *THROUGH TIME INTO HEALING*

Some past-life dreams are simply brief hypnogogic images that sometimes deal with death. In the following dream, Michael glimpsed a past life during a relaxation session at the end of a yoga class.

★ ★ ★

REVOLUTIONARY WAR

I was drifting off to sleep when I saw myself as a soldier with several other soldiers. We were all carrying rifles. The uniforms were from another time. I sensed it was the American Revolution. I'd no sooner glimpsed the image when an explosion of some sort ripped me apart. I watched the scenario dispassionately, even though I knew it was "me" who was killed. It was really vivid, a movie of the mind, and it ended with my death.

★ ★ ★

In Michael's case, the dream of being a soldier was startling, because in this life he had refused to serve in the Vietnam War, and had even been tried and convicted for his belief that the war was immoral. "Maybe my war experience in that other life affected my decision to avoid involvement in war in this life," he says.

The following past-life dream, recorded by Bernard, a librarian residing in South Florida, also provides a brief glimpse of another time and place, but it ends with a provocative scenario regarding access to reincarnational dreams.

★ ★ ★

A TRIP TO NINETEENTH-CENTURY LONDON

In the dream, I found myself on a street with horse-drawn carriages moving past me and sewers running down the edge of a road made of stone. The road was bordered by sooty brick buildings. I was dressed in heavy dark clothing of another era and wore a brimmed hat. I was definitely in another time and place and sensed it was mid-nineteenth-century London.

The dream faded, but I didn't wake up. Instead, I found myself in front of a panel with a horizontal row of red buttons. Although there was no writing, no instructions, I knew that each button represented a life in a different time. When I held my hand near one of the buttons, I knew instantly when and where the life took place. One was in ancient Egypt and another in Rome at the time of Christ. Still another took place in France during the Renaissance. All I had to do was push a button and I'd be there. I grew excited by the possibilities and that was when I woke up.

★ ★ ★

Bernard was skeptical about reincarnation and thought his dream might relate to his own interests. He maintains a strong interest in world history. Yet, when it was pointed out to him that his interest in history could be related to his past lives, he admitted that was a possibility. Bernard remains on the fence about the reality of past lives, but he is looking forward to dreaming again of the control panel and pushing the buttons.

Bernard's skepticism isn't surprising. In the West, in spite of a growing interest in the concept, reincarnation has not been widely accepted. The reason is at least partially related to the prevalent Judeo-Christian heritage. There is passing mention of reincarnation in the Old Testament and more references in the New Testament.

The turning point in Christianity's relationship to reincarnation appears to have taken place in the Second Council of Constantinople (the Fifth Ecumenical Council of the Church) in A.D. 553. One of the Council's fourteen anathemas, or denunciations, stated: "If anyone asserts the fabulous pre-existence of souls, and shall assert the monstrous restoration which follows it, let him be anathema."

Edgar Cayce, a devout Christian who popularized reincarnation in the United States in the early decades of the twentieth century through his clairvoyant readings, refused to debate whether the New Testament endorses or rejects the belief. As he put it: "I can read reincarnation into the Bible and you can read it right out."

HERBS

———————————— ■ ————————————

To dream of herbs means there will soon be pleasure in your life. To dream of poisonous herbs indicates your enemies are gossiping about you. A dream about useful herbs means satisfaction in business and warm friendships will soon be yours.

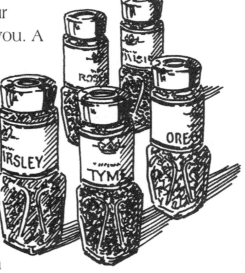

Dreaming of parsley means you will obtain success and be surrounded by healthy and lively people. To dream of eating parsley is a sign of good health.

The herb rosemary in a dream, on the other hand, portends sadness and indifference will cause unhappiness in your home, even though everything appears prosperous.

To dream of sage indicates thrift and economy will be practiced in your family. Women dreaming of sage will know a useless extravagance in love and fortune.

The resurgence of interest in past lives in recent decades can be attributed in part to writers such as Helen Wamback, Frederick Lenz, Ian Stevenson, Brian Weiss, and others.

Weiss's *Many Lives, Many Masters* spent months on the *New York Times* bestseller list. Here, after all, was a medical doctor and psychiatrist talking about a topic that had been largely relegated to the land of the weird and the strange. His books give the topic credence.

In *Through Time into Healing,* he describes a dream in which he was chained to a wall in a dungeon somewhere in Europe during the Middle Ages. He was tortured to death for teaching about reincarnation. While still in a hypnogogic state following the dream, he recalled another life in which he was a powerful priest at a ziggurat in the ancient Near East. He had abused his position for material gratification. Then he heard a voice speaking to him in a gentle, loving tone.

"When you had the chance to teach, you didn't. Then, when you didn't have the chance, you did. In that lifetime, you died for this belief when you didn't need to. You could have just as easily and successfully taught about love. At that moment, it wasn't right to force the issue. This time, get it right."

Weiss, however, is hardly the first Westerner to study reincarnation. In 1960, Dr. Ian Stevenson published a paper called "The Evidence for Survival from Claimed Memories of Former Incarnations." It consisted of forty-four cases that Stevenson had investigated personally, in which children identified enough details of their previous lives to identify the deceased persons who were supposedly reincarnated. Stevenson has spent most of the last three decades investigating the subject.

Reincarnation is one possible explanation for child prodigies. How could Mozart compose a symphony at the age of nine that was as good as or better than something written by a person who had studied music all his or her life? Was it just the luck of the draw, a random collision of the right genes? Or was it because his musical ability had been refined through many lives?

In early 1973, best-selling author Taylor Caldwell was questioned about her thoughts on reincarnation during an appearance at a book fair in Jacksonville, Florida. There was a great deal of interest in her visit—not only because of who she was, but because of who she might have been. Jess Stearn's *The Search for a Soul, the Psychic Lives of Taylor Caldwell* had been published recently and many of those who attended Caldwell's talk had read it.

When Caldwell asked for questions from the audience, the first one was whether or not she believed in reincarnation. She admitted that before she underwent the hypnotic regressions that constituted the background for Stearn's book, she'd been a die-hard skeptic. "Now I'm less skeptical," she said.

And yet, she had no way of explaining how she'd written so authentically of medical practices in ancient times, as she had in *Dear and Glorious Physician* and *Testimony of Two Men.* In *Physician,* for instance, there

is a surgery scene written with such breathtaking authenticity that Caldwell received letters from physicians all over the world, asking where she'd gotten her information.

None of these anecdotes, however, proves that we're born again. Ultimately, you have to settle that question for yourself. But it's interesting to note that regardless of our conscious belief or disbelief, our dreams sometimes point to what well may be previous lives.

In late 1974, when Christina was twenty-five years old, she began having a series of dreams that took place in Scotland. She'd never been there, but was planning a trip in the summer of 1975 with a woman coworker.

* * *

THE SCOTLAND DREAMS

These dreams were unlike any I'd ever had. They were vivid, in living Technicolor. They would often begin in the mountains that surround Caracas, Venezuela—where I was born—mountains that are so green the air there smells green. I would be running through all this green, racing toward the edge of a mountain, and then I would plunge over the edge and wildly flap my arms until I took to the skies. When I landed, I would be in Scotland.

I don't recall specific people or specific places in these dreams. But always, I awoke with the feeling that Scotland was as familiar to me as the rooms in my apartment.

As the trip to Scotland neared, the dreams increased in frequency and detail. They were like memories.

My friend and I spent six weeks in Europe and had set aside two weeks at the end just for Scotland. The day we boarded a bus for Edinburgh, I felt as though I were finally going home. As soon as I saw the city, I knew I'd lived there before.

It was the only city I've ever been in where I could walk down a particular street and know what I would find if I turned the corner. Most of the time, I was right. I remember sitting in a meadow of heather one night in early August, when the sky never got completely dark, and knowing with utter certainty that I'd often sat in a field of heather near here in another life. This wasn't fantasy to me; it was a clear, absolute knowing.

Before leaving Scotland, however, I felt that I had missed an opportunity, that there was something I was supposed to do or someone I was supposed to meet and somehow this event, whatever it was, hadn't happened. The feeling puzzled me, since the trip had surpassed my expectations.

* * *

Six years later, Christina was teaching English to Cuban refugees under a federal program to help Marielitos integrate into

Salt, pepper

Dreaming of salt generally signifies unhappy surroundings. To dream of eating salt portends that everything will go awry and quarrels will arise in your family circle. A young woman dreaming of eating salt indicates she will be deserted by her lover for a more beautiful woman. Ouch!

If you dream of pepper burning your tongue, you will suffer from your friends gossiping about you.

American life. A local reporter, Peter, visited the teaching center to find out how the program was going. Within five minutes of meeting him, Christina knew she'd met the man she would marry.

During the next year that they dated, Christina and Peter compared the parallels in their lives and travels. It turned out that Peter had been in Edinburgh during the same week in July 1975 that Christina had.

DREAMS & CHILDREN'S PAST LIVES

A fascinating new area of research involves the past lives of children. Author Carol Bowman, in her book *Children's Past Lives,* cites three distinct characteristics of dreams that may be related to a child's past lives:

★ Vivid and Coherent. This type of dream is often like a memory—clear and sharp in detail, with a fluid story line.

★ Recurring. Past-life dreams are often repetitive. "They usually start and stop in the same place in the story, like a video cued up to play the same segment over and over," writes Bowman.

★ Sometimes, these dreams revolve around a single image that the dreamer dreams in exactly the same way each time. Again, this image is like a memory. Other times, the dream progresses through a story line, then stops just short of a crisis point. Quite often, the crisis point is imminent death.

★ Different Personae. These are dreams in which the dreamer sees herself as another person in another time and place. "If that person is of a different sex or greatly different age, the dreamer,

upon awakening, knows that this dream was 'not like any dream I've ever had,'" Bowman writes.

★ Nightmares. Kids have nightmares that aren't past life memories, of course, but Bowman feels that some nightmares are "past-life memories screaming to be healed." These are the kind of nightmares from which a child awakens screaming night after night. Usually, the child heads for the parents' bed, crying for protection.

"What a difference it makes in our response if we look at nightmares as opportunities to heal past life traumas gripping the child." Even if a parent doesn't believe in reincarnation, she says, the nightmare shouldn't be brushed off as "it's only a dream." The child should be allowed to talk about it and the parents should listen with an open mind. "Unlike waking past life memories—which are already conscious—past life nightmares remain unconscious until your child talks about them while awake."

Exercise 24: MY PAST-LIFE DREAMS

List and describe three dreams you've had that took place in other time periods. Note what the people were wearing, what the landscape looked like, the mood of the dream, and the action. Did these dreams have a different feel to them than other dreams you've had? If so, how? Include as much description as possible. Were any of these dreams in response to a request for past-life information? If so, make a note of it.

Date of dream: .... Time period: ....

Description of dream: ....

....

....

....

....

Date of dream: .... Time period: ....

Description of dream: ....

....

....

....

....

Date of dream: .... Time period: ....

Description of dream: ....

....

....

....

....

Christina felt sure that her "missed opportunity" in Scotland was meeting Peter. They were married in July 1983, eight years after they missed meeting in Scotland.

"Destiny dictates the meeting of soulmates," writes Brian Weiss. "We *will* meet them. But what we decide to do after that meeting falls in the province of choice or free will. A wrong choice or a missed chance can lead to incredible loneliness and suffering. A right choice, an opportunity realized, can bring us to profound bliss and happiness."

Programming for Past-Life Dreams

Once you're able to consistently recall your dreams and are familiar with its language, you may find that some of your dreams or fragments of dreams involve scenes from times preceding your own birth. Brian Weiss believes these types of dreams are past-life memories.

In *Lifetimes, True Accounts of Reincarnation,* author Frederick Lenz isolates four ways in which dreams of past-life recall differ from ordinary dreams. According to Lenz, they usually entail sensations completely unlike those you experience in ordinary dreams, you're usually aware that you're seeing one or more of your past lives, you remember these dreams long after ordinary dreams have faded from your memory, and

past-life dreams tend to change the dreamer's attitudes toward death and dying.

Sometimes, as with the Scotland dreams, past-life dreams may precede a trip to a particular place and may intensify once you're in that place. Other times, such dreams may happen spontaneously, during periods of personal tension, anxiety, or tumult. Once you become proficient at recalling these dreams, you can program yourself to dream about your other lives. This is similar to the exercises presented earlier on dream incubation, but in this case you request dreams of past lives.

The next reincarnational dream began with an act of dream incubation. Before going to sleep, Anne asked herself why she and her husband were going through such a rocky period in their marriage. The answer was hardly what she had expected.

★ ★ ★

PRISON
I'm in a damp, musty-smelling room. The walls are stone, the floor is stone, and the air is dank. Very little light spills through the tiny window way up there near the ceiling. I realize I'm in prison.

But this isn't any contemporary prison. This is like something out of another century. I'm wearing a long dress that is tattered and soiled. I'm very young, maybe eighteen or nineteen, and I'm terrified.

One of the prison guards is nice to me. He brings me extra food. He talks to me. He consoles me with stories about the outside world. But sometimes, he's cold to me, he seems to feel guilty that he likes me. He says mean things to me, indifferent things. But then he'll try to make up for it with another gesture of kindness. I realize I'm going to die in this place and wake up with a choked, dry feeling in my throat.

★ ★ ★

The dream "clicked" for Anne. She knew the prison guard was her husband in this life and that she was the inmate. What struck her most about the dream was the vividness of the time period; it "felt" like the Middle Ages somewhere in England. Anne believed the dream was the vestige of a memory of a former life.

This certainly wasn't the kind of answer she'd asked for when she'd gone to sleep. But the dream explained facets of her marriage, and deepened her interest in reincarnation. Anne felt it also explained the acute discomfort she experienced when she traveled through England years before, a kind of choking gloom that clung to her until she left.

Her husband, not unexpectedly, remarked that the roles were reversed in this life. Although they joked about the dream, their relationship improved in the aftermath. "It was as if we became more aware of how we treated each other."

Michael Talbot, in *Your Past Lives*, recommends that you express your request in a clear, concise statement. Always tell your unconscious mind that you don't want to uncover any past-life memories that are too painful or traumatic to deal with. Talbot says he once forgot to add the qualifier when he'd requested a dream on a past-life injury. He was inundated with vivid nightmarish images and sensations about his death in a twelfth-century Persian war.

He suggests using a pendulum to find out if your request is safe to dream about. This entails nothing more than tying a small, weighted object like a ring to a piece of thread about ten inches long. With your elbow resting firmly on a flat surface, pinch the top of the thread between your thumb and forefinger and ask a question that has a yes answer. This establishes the direction the object will move when the answer is yes; the opposite direction means no. If the pendulum swings in a circle or moves diagonally, then rephrase the question. If you still can't obtain a clear answer, then it's best to leave that particular request alone for the time being.

As you're falling asleep, Talbot says, repeat your request several times. As with all dream recall, note your impressions of dreams the next morning, as soon as you awaken. A past-life dream, like any other dream, may be a literal visual experience or couched in symbolic terms.

If the dream doesn't make sense to you, let it alone for a while. Later, try the interviewing technique. Be alert for thoughts that may drift through your mind during the day. If the dream still hasn't made sense to you by that night, repeat your request, but change

SHAKESPEARE

—■—

To dream of William Shakespeare doesn't portend good luck— unhappiness and despondency will loom causing you much anxiety and your love will be stripped of passion.

If you dream of *reading* Shakespeare, however, you will attach yourself to literary accomplishments.

Romeo, Romeo, where for art though Romeo?

Exercise 25: BRAINSTORMING

This is a brainstorming session to find hidden talents and abilities you may have but haven't fully developed. Some of the questions you might ask yourself include the following:

☆　Are your hobbies and passions separate from your job or integrated into it?

☆　What kind of work would you like to do?

☆　What's holding you back from your heart's desire?

☆　How would you expand your present work/career?

☆　What is your "ideal" job or career?

UNDEVELOPED TALENTS AND ABILITIES

What I may want to work on:

What I would like to be doing:

Steps I can take toward this goal:

What I hope to achieve:

Now describe at least three dreams you've had that deal with abilities and talents that are now dormant in your life, but which you would like to develop.

TALENTS OF MY FUTURE SELF

Dream 1

Dream 2

Dream 3

the wording. Be specific, but make sure your wording covers what you want to know.

A good example of the importance of wording your request happened to Teresa, who was pregnant with her first child and wanted information on their past-life connection.

★ ★ ★

ICELAND

Before I went to sleep, I specifically asked for a dream that would tell me which life was the most important connection now for my husband and I and our unborn daughter. I dreamed I was in the early stages of labor and standing around in a giant warehouse, waiting for someone to help me. But the warehouse was empty of people and of furniture. There wasn't any place to lie down or even to sit.

The baby started to come out and I delivered her myself as I stood there. I remember holding her in my arms, astonished that the delivery had been so easy. She opened her eyes and said, in a very plain, clear voice, "Iceland."

When I woke up, I realized this was the exact answer to the request I had made. I'd asked which life, not for details of that life, and that's what I got. Iceland, a life in Iceland.

★ ★ ★

Dreams are your most personal and intimate way to explore your reincarnational history, but they aren't the only way. Meditation, hypnosis, and guided imagery all use altered states of consciousness to attain past-life information. And sometimes, of course, your waking life collides with someone else's, and there is an instantaneous recognition, as there was with Christina when she met Peter. Whatever course you choose, heed Brian Weiss's advice: "Listen to your heart, to your own intuitive wisdom . . ."

Past Lives Occurring Now

One of the primary differences between Seth's take on reincarnation and that of, say, Edgar Cayce, is that Seth views time—the past, the present, and the future—as existing simultaneously. In other words, all time exists in an eternal now; instead of a series of successive lives, one after another, your various lives are happening at the same time.

Since this would present obvious problems in physical reality as we know it, only one personality at a time is the focus personality. "Lives are simultaneous," Seth said in *The Unknown Reality*. "You can live more than one life at a time . . . but that is a loaded sentence. You are neurologically tuned in to one particular field of actuality that you recognize. You could not be consciously aware of those other realities all the time, and deal with the world that you know."

But the strengths and abilities of these other selves, says Seth, are available to you. And sometimes these talents become known to you in dreams. That was what happened to Paula, an elementary school teacher who, about five years into her career, began to have vivid dreams in which she was an artist.

★ ★ ★

THE ARTIST

As I approached the age of thirty I began to feel restless and unfulfilled as a teacher. I felt like I spent most of my time trying to maintain discipline in my classes. I was worn out by the time I left school every day and dreaded getting up in the morning because the whole cycle would start all over again. I wanted desperately to change careers, but didn't know what I would do.

In the midst of all this, I had a sequence of dreams in which I attended art classes. I learned how to draw, then to paint, and then to sculpt. These dreams refreshed me, so that when I got up in the morning, I was ready to deal with whatever happened at school. I was less uptight and conditions improved. But I realized I had to get out of teaching. So I enrolled in art classes.

Everything felt right about art. It was easy for me to learn, I loved doing it. Sculpture became my passion. When school was out, I attended an art institute for the summer. My sculptures began to sell—to family and friends, then by word of mouth to other people.

Two years later, I quit teaching for good and became a full-time sculptor.

Throughout this time, the dreams continued and evolved; they became more detailed. I realized these were period dreams, set in France around the time of van Gogh.

A few years later, I visited Arles, France, where van Gogh lived, and I felt a real kinship with the town. I don't think I was van Gogh, by any means, but I might have been a contemporary, and maybe a friend of his, another artist. Somehow, that artist life came to my aid when I needed it most.

★ ★ ★

Paula's case is fairly dramatic in that the dreams resulted in a change in career and a life change. More typical, perhaps, are the ways that abilities and strengths of past selves manifest in ordinary ways.

Sometimes you may have a flash of inspiration or an inexplicable hunch to do something that is totally out of character, but you do it because the intuition, the *nudge,* is so strong. In a sense, you have slipped into the state of mind that Australian Aborigines call Dreamtime, or what Seth refers to as imagination.

In *The Seth Material,* Seth says: "Imagination is waking man's connection with the dream system. Imagination often reinstates dream data and applies it to particular circumstances or problems within daily life . . ."

Future Lives

If time is plastic, if past, present, and future are happening simultaneously, then theoretically it should be possible to dream about who we will be. This phenomenor may be more common than you think.

In the early 1980s, Isabel had several dreams that involved a future society in Europe that lived under domes. In this future, she was a very tall, robust woman with a nearly bald head. She was terrified of what might exist outside of her domed world. She'd been taught that the world outside of the dome was toxic, and that one breath of the foul air would kill her.

She had recently begun to suspect, though, that the world external to the dome wasn't as terrible as the powers that be proclaimed. She began to view it as an impediment between herself and the truth.

In one of his readings, Edgar Cayce stated that he would be reborn in the twenty-first century, in the town of Billings, Montana, which would then be a waterfront town. Imagination? Wishful thinking? Maybe. But maybe not. If we are multidimensional beings, as Seth says, and have multidimensional talents to draw upon, then perhaps at some level we know who we will be tomorrow, or next year, or twenty years from now.

If nothing else, we should at least admit the possibility that we don't have all the answers, that despite our technology, we are in desperate need of new creeds and new paradigms to live by.

CHAPTER SEVENTEEN

The Dream Key

When stuck in traffic one afternoon, your mind wanders back to a friend you knew in college, whom you haven't seen or heard from in years. That night, out of the blue, this same person calls.

A couple go to the beach together, but soon get into a heated argument. At the peak of the argument, a bolt of lightning zig-zags across the sky, followed quickly by a crack of thunder. Before they can get away, a squall blows in and drenches them.

Coincidence? Not according to Carl Jung, one of the first to seriously study the seemingly random coinciding of events. In the Richard Wilhelm edition of the *I Ching*, Jung writes: ". . . synchronicity takes the coincidence of events in space and time as meaning something more than mere chance, namely a peculiar interdependence of objective events among themselves as well as with the subjective (psychic) states of the observer or observers."

The intent of this final chapter is to look at everyday life from a new perspective—the dream perspective. Synchronicity is one reminder that a subtle dreamlike quality underlies our waking lives.

> *We are in a time so strange that living equals dreaming, and this teaches me that man dreams his life, awake.*
>
> —CALDERON, *LIFE IS A DREAM*

Synchronicities are like road signs of the unconscious that point out certain patterns in our lives. As we become aware of them, we begin to notice more and more of them. We eventually learn to read these signs, what Brugh Joy calls "the pattern level of reality."

There were many instances of synchronicity in Jung's life, but one of the most vivid involved a beetle. As Jung was listening to a patient relate a dream in which she was given a golden scarab, he heard a tapping at the window and saw an insect fluttering against the glass. He opened the window and caught the insect. It was a scarabaeid beetle, the closest thing in his part of the world to a scarab. The scarab is a symbol of rebirth, and Jung interpreted this incident to mean the woman would now be helped by therapy.

Jung believed that synchronicity is inexorably linked to activation of energy deep within the psyche. "It is as if the formation of patterns within the unconscious mind is accompanied by physical patterns in the outer world," writes E. David Peat in *Synchronicity: The Bridge Between Matter and Mind*.

The most dramatic synchronicities seem to happen when people are undergoing a transition in their lives that leads to transformation—birth, falling in love, marriage, divorce, creative work, a switch in professions, a spiritual awakening. Sometimes long-

distance journeys can evoke these seemingly impossible "coincidences," as is the case in the following example provided by Jeffrey, an advertising executive.

* ★ ★ ★ *

ON THE BUS IN MOROCCO

It was the mid-1970s and I was traveling in Europe by myself. I only knew one person who was traveling in Europe at the time, but Frank was in Sweden, as far as I knew, and I was heading south. As I journeyed through France and Spain, I kept running into an Australian named Maurey, who was also traveling alone. Every time we met, we would greet each other, exchange a few words, and head on our individual ways, only to meet again.

One day, I decided to venture into Morocco and took a ferry from Gibraltar to Ceuta, a Moroccan border town. The scene was chaotic at the border and I was in a cultural shock—the Arabic language and writing, the style of dress, and even the music were all foreign and left me dazzled and confused.

But finally, I managed to get on a bus headed for a mountain village. As I found a seat I noticed a couple of other Westerners two rows in front of me. One of them turned and to my surprise, it was Maurey. Then I saw the other man's face. It was Frank, who I thought was in Sweden.

★ ★ ★

For Jeffrey, the series of synchronicities was important. He realized not only that there are hidden patterns in our lives but also that they're meaningful. He took the meaning of these synchronicities to be a message that no matter how isolated he felt, he was never alone.

Waking Life as a Dream

If you can step back from the dramas in your life and think of them as dreams, then you can interpret them the same way. By doing so, you can gain a new perspective on your life.

For Jim S., a reporter for a local television station in Iowa City, and his wife, a teacher, a broken garage door was initially merely an annoyance. Jim was attempting to get a new job with a station in a large metropolitan market and was frustrated by continual rejections. He knew he was ready to move on to a more prominent station, but the competition for those higher paying, prestigious positions was enormous.

Jim paid a repairman to put the door back on its track and forgot about it. But three weeks later, the door struck a ladder and was knocked off track again. That same day, a notice about a recall on the family minivan arrived in the mail. The bold lettering read: VERY IMPORTANT INFORMATION, and the letter went on to say that the lift-gate latch should be repaired.

Exercise 26: SYNCHRONICITIES IN MY LIFE

Record five instances of synchronicity that have happened to you—in your waking or dreaming life or both. Note if you found special meaning in these so-called coincidences, and how these events impacted your decisions or beliefs. If you can't recall any synchronicities from the past, watch for new incidents of synchronicity and record them as they occur.

Date: .... Time: ....

Circumstances: ....

....

....

....

Remarks: ....

....

....

....

★   ★   ★

Date: .... Time: ....

Circumstances: ....

....

....

Remarks: ....

....

....

....

Additional Remarks: ....

....

....

....

EXERCISE

Date: ....   Time: ....

Circumstances: ....

....

....

....

Remarks: ....

....

....

....

★   ★   ★

Date: ....   Time: ....

Circumstances: ....

....

....

....

Remarks: ....

....

....

....

★   ★   ★

Date: ....   Time: ....

Circumstances: ....

....

....

....

Remarks: ....

....

....

SPACE ALIEN

‑■‑

E T, Close Encounter of the Third Kind— if you dream that you encounter people from outer space and you feel strange around them, then strange things will start to happen in your life. If in your dream, however, you are positive toward the visitors from outer space, positive influences will be in your life. Care to take a trip to Roswell anyone?

That was when Jim noticed the symbolism. Doors. Big doors. Big openings. Problems with big openings. The minor annoyances reflected his life. But they were also easily repaired. It took only ten minutes for a repairman to fix the door, and an hour at the dealer to replace the latch. But how was he going to fix his career?

Three weeks after the second garage-door incident, Jim heard about an opening at a station in Philadelphia. It turned out the station manager was from Iowa City and familiar with his work. He got the job. After all the frustration, it was as easy as getting the garage door repaired.

Animal Symbols

While it might be easy to overlook the significance of a minor repair, as in the previous example, when a wild animal is involved, the incident is harder to ignore and the symbolism can be dramatic. That was the case when Anne, a Florida commercial artist, encountered a snake in her house.

★   ★   ★

SNAKE IN THE DEN
I was at the computer, updating my files. The sliding door to the atrium off the den was open because I'd just let my cat outside. Suddenly, I heard bushes rustling and my cat flew through the open door, chasing a snake.

It happened so fast, that for seconds I just sat there in a kind of paralysis. The only thing I could think of was that I was barefoot and the snake was under my desk.

Then I leaped up, grabbed my cat, and ran out of the den, shouting for my husband. He came running in with the broom. We didn't want to hurt the snake, but we didn't want the snake in the house, either.

We finally coaxed it near the door, but it darted between the glass door and the screen door and got trapped. It took us half an hour to get it out of the space between the doors and into the atrium.

Several days later, I found that it had shed its skin in the atrium.

Anne works with symbols and thinks in symbolic terms, so she immediately wondered what the snake experience meant. To figure it out, she turned to her Medicine Cards. These are divination cards that are based on Native American beliefs about the role of nature and animals in our lives. Although it wasn't a dream, the event transpired very much like a dream and that was how she chose to interpret it.

According to the Medicine Cards and certain Native American teachings, snakes represent transmutation. The shedding of the skin is the life/death/rebirth cycle, "the energy of wholeness." When snakes play a prominent role in an experience or dream or if you choose the snake card for yourself in a reading, it means that: ". . . there is a need within you to transmute some thought, action, or desire so that wholeness may be achieved."

The idea of transmutation "clicked" for Anne. At the time, she was dealing with the aging of her parents. Her mother had developed a short-term memory problem and it was a tremendous strain on her father. Two days after the experience with the snake, her father was rushed to the hospital with a high fever and abdominal pain that was diagnosed as diverticulitis. Her mother was so disoriented by his absence that Anne didn't want to leave her alone, so she stayed with her. This was when she realized the extent of her mother's memory loss.

Anne believed the snake symbolized the transmutation that had to occur in her own thoughts concerning her parents. She had to accept the reality that they were aging and weren't going to live forever.

The Naskapi

In many primitive cultures, the distinction between dreams and waking life was much less defined than it is today in the Western world. The dream life and the waking life were closely related and even flowed together. The Naskapi are an example of one such culture, which still lives on.

The Naskapi Indians inhabit an inhospitable region in northeastern Canada. There are about three hundred members of the tribe, which has no government or institutions

CHURCH AND SYNAGOGUE

If you dream of seeing a church off in the distance, a long awaited event will be disappointing. Dreaming of entering a church in a gloomy mood can mean you should expect some sadness in the near future.

If you dream of seeing a synagogue off in the distance, it means your enemies are preventing you from acquiring a fortune. If you climb to the top of the outside of the synagogue, you soon will overcome any opposition to you.

One would think dreaming of houses of worship would indicate peace and happiness. But the world of dreams can be surprising!

Exercise 27: CIRCLE

A circle has been divided into twelve equal parts, each part represents an aspect of life. Outside of each part, write two observations about patterns pertaining to that part of your life. The twelve areas are:

The self: the physical body and your feelings about your body, as well as how you project yourself to others.
Finances: Money. Possessions and earning ability.
Siblings: Brothers and sisters. If you're an only child, then this area pertains to people who are like siblings to you.
Mother and home: all things related to your relationship with your mother and to your home.
Children and creativity: This part includes any creative pursuit, regardless of whether you make money at it.
Health and work: If you're involved in charity work, include it here.

Partnerships: all close partnerships—romantic, business, etc.
Sexuality: how you feel about yourself sexually.
Spiritual beliefs: everything pertaining to religious, philosophical, and spiritual beliefs goes here.
Father and profession: all things related to your relationship with your father and to your feelings about your profession and career.
Friends and associates: the people around you, the people you work with, and the groups and associations you belong to all go here.
Dreams, hopes, and wishes: all that you wish to attain.

Once you've completed your comments, focus on those that seem negative or that make you uncomfortable. Then, go to Exercise 28, rewrite them in a positive way.

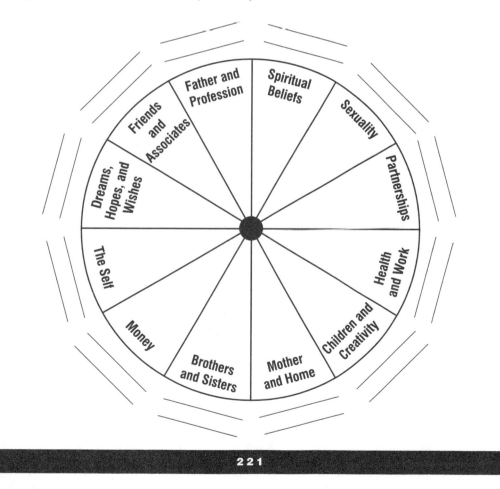

and no organized religion. Life is centered around hunting caribou and bear and the tribe's rich, spiritual environment.

"Central to the life of the Naskapi," writes David Peat in *Synchronicity,* "is the Big Dream, in which the hunter goes on the trail, meets friends, and locates herds of caribou." Once the hunter wakes from the dream, he will quite often start drumming and chanting to communicate the dream to those around him. In this way, the spirits of the animals in the bush are alerted to the dream.

According to the beliefs of the Naskapi, a hunter's dreams will become clearer and more powerful if he respects the animals and other members of his tribe. If he violates this code of respect, his dreams will desert him.

In conjunction with dreams, the Naskapi also use various forms of divination, including a bone oracle. The greatest diviners in the tribe are those who are in deepest harmony with the Manitou, or spirit of the animals. After tossing a bone into a fire, they study the cracks and dark spots for information on everything from trails to the location of herds.

The survival of the tribe depends on each hunter's ability "to recognize patterns and flux of nature and to live in harmony with them," Peat notes. Through the bone oracle and dreams, the hunter maintains contact with the Manitou. "The Naskapi live in a world of meaningful pattern in which no distinction exists between what we have come to call mind and matter," Peat notes.

Lessons from the Naskapi

For the Naskapi people, the recognition and understanding of patterns is a way of life. Think about the events in your current life. Try to think of your life as a dream and interpret the events in it using the same techniques you've learned in the earlier chapters. You might interview yourself to uncover the meaning of the events. Be alert for symbols or significant images or words.

Are there any dramas in your life that are repeated over and over? Consider these events as similar to recurring dreams. If you're single, do your relationships tend to follow the same path? If you're married, do the same issues keep coming up again and again? Do your kids consistently do well in school or do they get into trouble? Is money flowing into your life or are you facing recurring money problems? Is your career flourishing or are you unsatisfied with it? Is your health consistently good or are you chronically ill? Does your car run smoothly or does it keep breaking down?

All of these things are patterns, the internal made manifest. By learning to recognize, interpret, and work with the patterns that operate in your life, you can become better able to control and shape your destiny.

For example, if you wrote: "My money goes out as fast as it comes in," you might rewrite it as: "Money flows into my life." In essence, you're creating an affirmation, a statement about a condition that doesn't exist yet but which you would like to manifest in your life. You can also practice working with these new statements, these *new patterns,* in your dreams by using them as suggestions before going to sleep.

The following example of Exercise 28 was completed by Lynn, a thirty-five-year-old woman in the entertainment business.

Patterns Lynn wants to create:

1. The Self:
   ☆ My weight is perfect
   ☆ I love and appreciate myself.

2. Money:
   ☆ New money projects pour into my life.
   ☆ I am open to universal abundance.

3. Brothers & sisters:
   ☆ Things are good.

4. Mother and home:
   ☆ Things are fine.

5. Children and creativity:
   ☆ I tap the deepest sources of my creativity.
   ☆ My ideas and the ways I implement them flow without effort.

6. Health and work:
   ☆ My work opportunities multiply.
   ☆ I seize the opportunities and turn them into projects that satisfy me and that I enjoy working on.

7. Partnerships:
   ☆ I attract partnerships that are equal and fair.
   ☆ I am open to romantic partnerships with men that are happy and fulfilling.

8. Sexuality:
   ☆ I feel fine about myself.

9. Spiritual beliefs:
   ☆ I integrate my spiritual beliefs with my work, so that my work becomes a reflection of those beliefs.
   ☆ I actively pursue a deepening in my spiritual awareness.

10. Father and profession:
    ☆ My career takes off: it goes into orbit.
    ☆ Professionally, I am exactly where I always dreamed I would be.

11. Friends and associates:
    ☆ I get along well with people.

12. Dreams, hopes, and wishes:
    ☆ I find my right path.
    ☆ I feel personally empowered.

Exercise 28: MY PATTERNS

Once you've completed your comments in Exercise 27, focus on those that seem negative or that make you uncomfortable. Then rewrite them here in a positive way.

Patterns I want to create

Self:

Money:

Brothers and sisters:

Mother and home:

Children and creativity:

Health and work:

Partnerships:

Sexuality:

Spiritual beliefs:

Father and profession:

Friends and associates:

Dreams, hopes and wishes:

Notes:

PART FOUR

A Dream
Glossary

CHAPTER EIGHTEEN

Dream
Interpretations

Through the various exercises in this book, you may already have built an impressive glossary of your personal definitions for symbols that have appeared in your dreams. If there are still symbols that puzzle you, however, this glossary may trigger ideas that "click" for you.

When you first begin interpreting symbols and themes in your dreams, work with your own dream symbols first, rather than immediately turning to this glossary. Take note of details in your dreams—colors, vividness, the action, or anything unusual that stands out. If you dream of a particular animal, for instance, associate it with situations and conditions in your life, institutions that you deal with, or people you know well.

When it comes to dreams, there are no universal rules or meanings. Keep that in mind when you use this glossary. Also, note that some dreams might be a literal message of something that is about to happen to you, rather than a symbolic message. A dream scenario might also relate to scenes from a past life. Although such interpretations might be rare, they are worth considering.

> *. . . learning to understand our dreams is a matter of learning to understand our heart's language.*
>
> —ANN FARADAY,
> *THE DREAM GAME*

A

Abdomen Seeing your abdomen in a dream suggests the gestation or digestion of a new idea or phase of your life. If your abdomen is swollen, the birth of a new project may be imminent.

Actor or Actress Perhaps you're only seeing your own or someone else's persona, the side the person shows to the world. Seeing yourself as an actor in the spotlight suggests a desire for publicity or a more public life. Such a dream can also suggest that you're acting out a role or "putting on an act" for someone else.

Afternoon Dreams that take place in the afternoon suggest clarity and lengthiness of duration. Are you with friends in the afternoon? Then positive and lasting associations may soon be formed.

Airplane You may be soaring to new heights in some facet of your life or taking a metaphorical journey into the unconscious. An airplane dream can also be a prelude to a flying dream or used as a launch pad to a lucid dream.

Alligator This symbol may suggest that you're being thick-skinned or insensitive to someone else. It may also signify danger.

Amusement Park Dreaming of an amusement park may suggest that you are in need of a vacation from your concerns over a troubling issue. To dream of riding a ride denotes an enjoyment of life and feelings of being uninhibited.

Anchor An anchor grounds you—acts as your foundation. It also holds you in place, which can be either beneficial or detrimental.

Angels Angels represent help from the higher self or from a guardian. The appearance of an angel may suggest a growing spiritual awareness.

Animals Animals can relate to various sides of your "animal" nature, a guardian spirit, wisdom, innocence, predatory tendencies, or sexuality, depending on the perceived nature of the animal. An animal can also represent the physical body, or appear as a metaphor for an illness within the physical body.

Ant Ants suggest restlessness (feeling "antsy"). They also signify small annoyances and irritations. Alternately, they may represent feelings of smallness or insignificance. Consider the number of ants in the dream. Is it a single ant? A colony? Or a huge, swollen anthill?

Apparition An apparition can signify a message or warning. It can be seen as communication with the dead. Alternately, you might feel that another person in a relationship is like an apparition—someone who is there, but not truly present.

Apples Apples stand for wholeness and for knowledge. Ripe apples on a tree may mean that your hope and hard work have borne fruit.

April As April showers lead to May flowers, to dream of this month represents that much pleasure and fortune may be heading your way. If the weather is bad, it may suggest the passing of bad luck.

Arch Passing under an arch in a dream may symbolize a transition in your life, a move from one phase or stage to another. If you avoid walking under the arch, the indication is that you are resisting transition or change. Note the shape of the arch, whether it's adorned in any way, or whether other people are also using it. This will flesh out the symbol for you.

Arm Arms allow you to manipulate things in your environment. The same might be true in a dream. Seeing an arm suggests that you can maneuver or manipulate things in your dream environment. If you flap your arms, it may indicate a desire to fly in your dream.

Atlas Dreaming of an atlas suggests that you are considering moving or taking a trip.

Attic If you dream of entering an attic, you may be exploring the realm of the higher self or seeking knowledge there. An attic can also suggest a place where things are hidden or stored from the past. The dream might be suggesting that you take some part of you out of hiding or that you should dispose of the things you are clinging to from your past.

August Dreaming of August may suggest unfortunate dealings in business and love. A young woman dreaming that she will be wed in this month is an omen of sorrow in her early married life.

B

Baby A baby in a dream may represent an idea that is gestating or growing. It could also relate to the pending birth of a child or a desire for a family. Alternately, a baby could indicate dependent behavior or infantile longings. A baby walking alone indicates independence. A bright, clean baby represents requited love and many warm friends.

Balcony A balcony might stand for the public part of the personality. Consider the condition of the balcony. If it's clean and polished, the dream indicates that you are held in high regard by others. If it's a crumbling, tarnished balcony, it may suggest that you need to repair your public image.

Bank Generally, a bank is a symbol of security and power—a foundation—but the meaning depends on what you're doing in the bank. If you are receiving or depositing money, it's usually an auspicious sign, an indication that you are financially secure. If you are waiting in line, it literally may mean waiting for a check or money to arrive. Likewise, if you're holding up a bank, it may symbolize that money you're expecting is being "held up" or delayed.

Basement Dreaming of being in a basement could indicate that you are connecting with the subconscious mind. Possibly you are unearthing something hidden in your past that you need to examine. (see Underground.)

Bathroom Dreaming of being in a bathroom could simply mean that your bladder is full. It could also symbolize a place of privacy. If the bathroom is crowded, the dream could mean that you lack privacy. If you find yourself in a bathroom for the opposite sex, it may suggest that you are crossing boundaries. A bathroom dream may also relate to the elimination of something in your life.

Birds The appearance of a bird in a dream could relate to a wish for freedom, to

BIRDS OF PREY

There is a scheming person out to injure you if you dream of vultures. But this evildoer will not succeed if you dream the vulture is dead. A woman dreaming of a vulture indicates she will soon be overwhelmed by slander and gossip.

If you dream of a buzzard, also watch out. An old scandal is likely to surface and injure your reputation. And if you dream of a buzzard sitting on a railroad, you might experience an accident or loss in the near future.

Should the buzzard in your dream fly away, all your troubles will be resolved!

fly away, or to flee from something. Birds can also be spiritual symbols. Among certain Native American tribes, an eagle symbolizes spiritual knowledge. A vulture might symbolize death and a hummingbird might point to a matter accelerating or to the tendency to flit from one thing to another.

Birthday Birthday dreams can have contrary meanings depending on the context. To dream of receiving birthday presents may mean happy surprises or advancements are in order. For an older person to dream of a birthday may signify long hardship and sorrow; to the young it is a symbol of poverty.

Bleeding Blood is vital to life, and to dream of bleeding suggests a loss of power and a change for the worse in fortune.

Breasts Women's breasts may relate to sexual desire. They can also symbolize nurturing, motherhood, or a concern about exposure. Are the breasts exposed? Are they diseased or injured? Always consider what's going on in relation to the symbol.

Bridge Since a bridge connects us from one place to another, in dreaming it may represent a crossing from one state of mind to another. Consider the other elements in the dream. Are you crossing dangerous waters? What's waiting for you at the other side of the bridge? What's behind you?

Bus A bus can be a vehicle for moving ahead to one's goal. If you're trav-

eling with others, you could be on a collective journey. Notice other aspects of the dream, such as the luggage you're carrying, your destination, and what you're leaving behind.

C

Cage A cage represents possession or control, and what you see in the cage is the key to interpreting this sign. A cage full of birds may signify great wealth and many children, while a single bird may represent a successful marriage or mate. An empty cage may mean the loss of a family member, while a cage full of wild animals may signify that you have control over a particular aspect of your life and that you will triumph over misfortune.

Cake A cake might symbolize that a celebration is at hand. Or perhaps there's something to celebrate that has been overlooked.

Canal Canals suggest a journey through the unconscious. Pay attention to other details in the dream. Is the water muddy or clear? Are you traveling with friends or family?

Cancer Dreaming of cancer doesn't mean you have it or are going to get it. To be successfully treated for cancer in a dream signals a change for the better.

WADING, WALKING, RUNNING

Wading: If you dream of wading in clear water expect joy. To dream of wading in muddy water, however, means that you will experience sorrow. For a young woman to dream of wading in clear water means she will have her hearts desire. And to dream of children wading signifies future happiness.

Walking: A dream of walking in the woods means you will have business difficulties. Dreaming of walking at night means you will have struggle and difficulty. But dreaming of walking in pleasant places indicates good fortune and favor.

Running: If you dream of running, not from a predator, but running for exercise, that means that you are moving toward a pleasant and successful life.

Dreaming of cancer may symbolize a desperate or foreboding situation, or a draining of resources.

Candles Usually something of a spiritual nature is suggested by the appearance of candles. A candle provides light in the dark, or guidance through dark matters or through the unknown. If a candle burns down to nothingness, it might indicate a fear or concern about death or impotence. A candle being put out could indicate a feeling of being overworked. A steadily burning candle may signify a steadfast character and constancy in friends and family.

Canoe Canoes suggest a short journey that requires some effort, but that is often pleasantly tranquil. Pay attention to other elements in the dream, such as the state of the water and how hard you are paddling. A dream of paddling on a calm stream symbolizes confidence in your own abilities. If the river is shallow and quick, the dream may indicate concern over a hasty decision in a recent matter. To dream of rowing with your paramour may indicate an imminent and lasting marriage, but if the waters are rough, then perhaps some effort is required before you are ready to marry.

Car A moving car may mean you are headed toward a goal or moving ahead. If you're in the driver's seat, a car can symbolize taking charge of your life. Is there a "backseat driver" in the vehicle? Or are you taking the backseat in some situation in your life? Being a passenger indicates that someone else might be controlling a situation. A stolen or lost car could indicate that you are losing control of your life. Cars sometimes represent the physical body, so take note of the car's condition. Is it rusting? Does the exterior shine? How does the interior look?

Carousel To dream of riding a carousel suggests that you are going round in circles and not making any progress in your endeavors. Seeing others ride a carousel symbolizes unfulfilled ambitions.

Castle Seeing one of these majestic structures in a dream might suggest power and strength, security and protection. Castles in the sky are fantasies and illusions, wishes to escape from one's present circumstances.

Cat Cats can have both positive and negative attributes, depending on your association with cats and the surrounding circumstances in the dream. Cats can mean prosperity; kittens can mean new ideas. Kittens in a basement could be ideas arising from the unconscious mind. Cats can represent independence, the feminine, or sexual prowess. They can also stand for evil or bad luck, or a catty or cunning person.

Cattle To dream of healthy, content cattle grazing in a green pasture suggests prosperity and happiness. Conversely,

dreaming of weak, poorly fed cattle suggests you are misspending your energy. Stampeding cattle implies that something in your life is out of control.

Cellar   A cellar often symbolizes the unconscious mind, a place where knowledge is stored or hidden. It can also indicate that the dream comes from the deepest levels of your unconscious, so pay special attention to the way the cellar is lit and to colors and textures.

Chariot   Riding in a chariot in a dream suggests positive news or success in a matter.

Children   By dreaming of children, you possibly may yearn to return to a simpler, less complicated life. Such dreams might also relate to a desire to return to the past to recapture good times or to satisfy unfulfilled hopes.

Chocolate   Chocolate suggests a need or a desire to indulge in something, perhaps a forbidden something. It also can indicate a need to limit your indulgences.

Circle   A circle in Jungian terms represents the Self, wholeness. It can also relate to a symbol of protection or social connections, as in a "circle" of friends. If you're "circling around something," caution is indicated. Finally, the Freudian interpretation is that the circle represents the vagina and sexual desire.

Closet   Closets are places where things are stored or hidden. If there is something you are hiding in your life, your dream possibly may indicate that it is time to release whatever it is.

Clouds   Dark, stormy clouds rolling in at a low altitude and flashing lightning may represent your anger regarding a situation. A slate gray clouded sky might indicate that your views are clouded on a subject. What is it in your life that needs clarity? Dreaming of white, billowing clouds floating in a blue sky suggests that matters are clearing up.

Coffin   A coffin may symbolize a feeling of confinement. Coffins also relate to death; ask yourself what part of your life might be dead.

College   College represents distinction and the attainment of your hopes through hard work. To dream of a college may suggest that you will advance to a position long sought after. Dreaming that you are back in college suggests that distinction will follow a period of hard work.

Corpse   To dream of yourself as a corpse or to experience your death is not necessarily a prediction of your demise. It could signify a major change in your life, such as the ending of a long-held job or a divorce. If you dream of killing yourself, it could mean that you are going through a traumatic personal transformation, leaving your old life behind.

Cow   A cow can represent fertility, sustenance, or even prosperity. Alternately, a cow might signify a desire for sexual intercourse, or a fear of being unable to resist engaging in sex.

Creek   A creek represents a short journey or a new experience. Are you exploring a creek with a friend? Is the creek muddy? Note the other aspects of the dream.

Crown   The obvious definition is wealth, position, power, and authority. But is the crown something desired or feared in the dream? Is it within reach or escaping your grasp?

D

Dancing   A dream dance evokes movement, freedom, joy, and a time of happiness and levity.

Darkness   Darkness is a symbol of the unconscious, the hidden, and the unknown. Darkness can also stand for evil, death, and fear. To dream of being overtaken by darkness suggests fear or trepidation over a matter at hand. To dream that you lose a friend or child in the darkness symbolizes that you may be provoked from many different sources.

Daybreak   Daybreaks symbolize that the outlook is brightening on a matter. A gloomy or cloudy day suggests bad luck in a new enterprise.

Dead   The appearance of the dead in a dream typically signifies a warning of some kind. To see the dead living and happy represents a bad influence that may be affecting your life.

Death   A death dream usually isn't a premonition of death, but it may indicate a death. If there's no sense of fear in the death, the dream can mean you're letting go of something, moving on. On the other hand, a corpse can indicate a lifeless routine.

December   A time of gift giving and receiving, to dream of this month can suggest the accumulation of wealth and fortune.

Deer   A deer in a dream may symbolize hunting. Deer are also graceful and gentle creatures, easily frightened. In folklore, deer are the messengers of fairies and therefore could be seen as messengers of the unconscious.

Desert   A desert is usually thought of as a barren place, where little grows. It can be symbolic of a fear of death, or of being barren. But a desert can also symbolize hidden beauty and hidden life that is camouflaged to ordinary perceptions.

Dew Suggestive of tiny treasures or small pleasures, to dream of sparkling dew may represent that wealth and achievement are due. For a single person, perhaps a fortunate marriage is imminent.

Diamond A diamond symbolizes love, as in a diamond ring, and money. A lost diamond, especially a ring, may symbolize a concern about a love relationship. A gift of a diamond depends on who's giving it and other circumstances. A diamond from a parent or relative could relate to an inheritance; one from a friend might indicate a wish to obtain the person's love.

Digging What are you digging for? If it's something lost, you may be attempting to retrieve a part of your past. If it's a treasure, you may be delving into the unconscious, a treasure-house of knowledge. If, however, you are burying something, it indicates a wish to cover up an act, hide your feelings, or hide the facts of the matter.

Diving To dream of diving into a body of water may indicate that you are about to dive into something related to your waking life. On a deeper level, a diving dream may symbolize an exploration of the unconscious. From a Freudian perspective, such a dream suggests the dreamer is diving into a new sexual relationship.

Doctor A doctor can indicate a healing or healing guide. For some people, a doctor in a dream might symbolize main-

stream thinking as opposed to alternative health options.

Dog Dreaming of a dog can mean that you're seeking companionship, affection, or loyalty. If the dog bites, it might indicate a feeling of disloyalty. To hear dogs barking suggests a message or a warning from your unconscious.

Dolphins A dolphin may be considered a messenger of the unconscious, since it resides in the sea. Perhaps the dolphin is a guide to the unconscious realms, which may suggest that you are diving into the unconscious.

Door A common dream symbol, doors can indicate an opening or a new opportunity at hand. A closed door suggests that something is inaccessible or hidden. If a door is broken, there may be something hindering you from the new opportunity. The condition of the door, the material it's made of, and any markings that appear on it often provide clues about what lies behind a closed door.

Drinking Drinking water in a dream might simply mean that you are thirsty. Symbolically, water is related to the unconscious and emotions. Drinking may suggest you are being nourished or have a thirst for emotional involvement. Drinking alcoholic beverages can symbolize a sense of feeling high about a matter. As a metaphor, the drinking of "spirits" may suggest a search for spiritual sustenance. For an alcoholic or someone close to an alcoholic, a dream of drinking alcohol might be a warning.

Drought   Generally an unfavorable omen in a dream, droughts represent the absence of life or the drying up of your emotions. Are you with someone in the dream? Then maybe there is an unresolved issue between you and someone you are close to that is leading to a quarrel or separation.

Drum   Dreaming of a drum or drumbeats might relate to a primitive urge. Alternately, a drum possibly symbolizes communication, magic, or even an entrepreneurial spirit—as in drumming-up business.

Dusk   Dusk denotes the end of the day; the end of happiness or clarity on an issue, or a dark outlook on a matter at hand.

Dwarf   Dwarfs are traditionally associated with magical powers. Dreaming of a dwarf could be an extremely fortuitous sign. On the other hand, a dwarf can symbolize a stunted condition. If growth is limited, alternate paths must be pursued.

Dying   Dreams of dying represent the ending of an emotional state or situation at hand. To dream that you are going to die suggests an inattention to a particular aspect of your life. To see animals in the throes of death symbolizes bad influences are a threat.

E

Eagle   The eagle, soaring through the sky, can symbolize a spiritual quest. The bird can also stand for combat, pride, courage, and ferocity. Eagles traditionally were associated with nobility. They also can symbolize a father figure or the sun.

Ears   To dream of human ears can be a warning to watch out what you say. Ears can also call attention to the need to listen carefully to what's going on around you.

Earthquake   Dreaming of an earthquake might suggest that personal, financial, or business matters are unstable. Is there something upsetting taking place in your life? Earthquakes can also have sexual connotations, such as the desire for sexual release. If there are others in the dream, does one of them make the "earth move" for you?

Eating   A dream of eating might suggest a desire or craving for love or power. It can mean you are enjoying life or indulging in its pleasures. If you are the one being eaten in the dream, ask yourself if something is "eating at you." Do you feel as if you are being eaten alive?

Eclipse An eclipse suggests a disruption of the normal. When something is "eclipsed," it signifies a period of activity has ended. Also, an eclipse can mean that cosmic forces may be at work in your life.

Eel An eel can be a phallic symbol. Its movement through waters contains sexual overtones. Take your cues from what the eel is doing.

Egg In the Freudian interpretation, eggs can symbolize the male testicles and stand for virility. In the Jungian view, eggs represent wholeness, fertility, and new life. Eggs can also represent unhatched ideas; finding a nest of eggs might indicate a waiting period, or that ideas are gestating. What is the context of the dream? Is someone "egging" you on?

Elephant The appearance of these large, solid animals may portend the possession of wealth, honor, and a steadfast character. As the elephants rule in the wild, their appearance in your dream may suggest that you reign supreme in business and at home. How many elephants are you seeing? A herd of elephants may suggest great wealth, while a single elephant may represent a small but solid life.

Elevator Rising in an elevator may symbolize a raising of status, such as a promotion, or a raising of consciousness. Is the ascent rapid? Are you frightened? Exhilarated? A descent in an elevator might indicate a lowering in status or position, or a journey into the unconscious. Keep in mind that the dream might indicate hopes or fears rather than actual events. A stuck elevator might suggest that some aspect of your life is presently stuck. A plunging elevator could indicate a rapid descent into the unconscious.

Escaping If you dream of making an escape, consider whether you are avoiding something in your life, or whether you need to get away from something.

Evening A dream that takes place in the evening suggests uncertain or unrealized hopes. To dream of stars shining suggests present troubles followed by brighter times. A dream of lovers walking in the evening symbolizes separation.

Evergreen A dream of an evergreen—especially the word itself—might suggest a metaphor. To be "evergreen" indicates wealth or at least financial stability. An evergreen or pine tree might also indicate hope or even immortality. A decorated evergreen or Christmas tree suggests giving or receiving gifts.

HEARING VOICES

Dreaming that you are hearing pleasant voices indicates joyous reconciliations will happen in your future. If the voices are angry, expect disappointments; if the voices are weeping, expect to have a sudden outburst of anger.

If you hear the voice of God, honorable people will soon praise you for your unselfishness and generosity.

If you dream of a ventriloquist, on the other hand, beware of deception and fraud. Dreaming of a ventriloquist can also mean that a love affair could turn out bad for you.

Examination If you dream of taking an exam, it might indicate a concern about failure. A stack of tests could suggest you feel you are being tested too often. Look at the surrounding elements in the dream. If you forgot to go to class, the dream suggests that you are worried about being unprepared.

Explosion A dream of an explosion could be an attempt by your unconscious to get your attention to a matter of concern. An explosion could suggest a release or an outburst of repressed anger, or an upheaval in your life.

F

Falling Falling is a common dream symbol and usually an expression of a concern about failure. The dream could be a metaphor for falling down on the job. In most falling dreams, the dreamer never lands. If you do hit the ground, it could mean that you've struck bottom in a matter. If you get up unhurt, the dream may be suggesting that you won't be hurt by something that you perceive as a failure.

Fat A dream of being fat might be a concern about your diet, but it could also be a metaphor for wealth and abundance, or overindulging.

Father The appearance of your father can have many connotations, depending on

the context of the dream and your relationship with him. Typically it represents a need for advice over a troubling situation.

Father-in-Law To dream of your father-in-law suggests strife with friends or a family member. To see him happy and well augurs pleasant family relations.

Feather To dream of a feather floating through the air bodes well. Your burdens will be light and easily borne. To dream of an eagle feather implies that your aspirations will be met.

February A dream of this short, winter month suggests continued ill health and melancholy. To dream of a sunshiny day in this month may suggest an unexpected change in fortune and outlook.

Fence A dream of a fence can indicate that you feel "fenced in." A fence can block you or it can protect you. If you are "on the fence," the dream might suggest that you are undecided about something.

Fever To dream that you are suffering from a fever suggests a needless worry over a small affair.

Fight To fight in a dream may represent a conflict or the need to resolve an issue. Pay attention to other details in the dream in order to interpret it. Are you winning or losing a fight? Are you fighting with a loved one?

Fire   Fire is generally a favorable symbol to the dreamer, as long as he or she is not burned, representing continued prosperity and fortune. If you're on fire, it's probably a metaphor for passion; it's as if you are burning with desire. Alternately, fire can symbolize destruction, a purification, illumination, and a spiritual awakening. Look at other metaphors: What are you getting "fired up" about? Are you (or another figure in the dream) concerned about "being fired" or "getting burned"?

Fire Engine   A symbol of distress and ultimately of protection, to dream of a fire engine indicates worry over an important matter at hand that will soon be resolved.

Fire Fighting   To dream of fighting flames suggests that hard work is required before success in a matter at hand is achieved. To dream of a fire fighter may suggest solid friendships. To dream of an injured fire fighter indicates that a close friend may be in danger.

Fireworks   A dream of fireworks suggests a celebration, a joyous explosion, or a release of repressed feelings.

Fish   Fish swimming symbolize exploration of the unconscious or that which lies below the surface. In the Freudian interpretation, fish are phallic symbols and dreaming of fish is related to sexual desires. The Jungian interpretation is that fish symbolize a spiritual quest or seeking.

Flood   A dream of a flood might suggest that you are being overwhelmed by a rising awareness of the unconscious aspects of your being. A dream of flooding can also serve as a warning that personal matters are spilling over into other areas of your life. Alternately, a flood can relate to a release of sexual desires or a need to do so.

Flower   Flowers in a dream can symbolize love and beauty. Flowers can also be a symbol of the inner self. New blossoms suggest the opening of the inner self. Withered and dead flowers can mean disappointment and dismal situations.

Flying   A flying dream may suggest the dreamer is soaring, or "flying high" as a result of a successful venture. Flying can also symbolize breaking free of restrictions or inhibitions. But flying itself can be a joyous experience in a dream no matter what the symbolic meaning.

Fog   Dreaming of foggy conditions indicates a lack of clarity in some aspect of your life. Fog can also symbolize something hidden or something you're not seeing. Keep in mind that fog is usually short-lived and when it lifts, you will gain a new sense of clarity.

Forest A forest suggests an exploration of the unconscious. It also can symbolize a need or desire to retreat from everyday life, to restore and revitalize your energies. To dream of a lush forest in complete foliage may mean prosperity and pleasure, whereas finding yourself in a dense forest may signify unpleasantness at home. A forest fire may symbolize the successful completion of your plans, with wealth and prosperity to follow.

Fountain A dream of a fountain can suggest longevity and virility. Water is related to the emotions and unconscious, so a fountain can indicate an emotional surge. Alternately, a dream of a fountain can indicate an examination of your emotions. What is the condition of the fountain? A clear fountain suggests vast possessions and many pleasures. A dry and broken fountain symbolizes the end of pleasure. A sparkling fountain in the moonlight can indicate an ill-advised pleasure.

Frog Frogs, like the prince who was turned into one, are transformative creatures. They start as tadpoles, grow legs and arms, and develop lungs. To dream of a frog may imply a major change or transformation in your life. Since frogs live part of their lives in water, a frog may also symbolize a leap into the unconscious.

Frost Frost, like ice, may represent an emotional state of the dreamer or a person in the dream. To see a friend or lover in frost could mean chilly feelings regarding the relationship.

G

Gambling Dreaming of gambling suggests taking a chance. If you are winning, it may bode well for a risky business deal. If you're watching others win, the game may symbolize a fear of taking a chance. Whether you should be more daring or play it safe depends on other factors in the dream.

Garbage To dream of garbage suggests a need to get rid of old, worn out ideas, or excess baggage in your life. Ask yourself if you are clinging to something or some condition that you no longer need?

Garden A garden sometimes indicates a need to bring more beauty into your life. It may be a metaphor for personal or spiritual growth, or a desire to cultivate a new talent or move into a higher realm of awareness. A garden with lots of weeds may symbolize a need to weed out old, outmoded ideas or a desire to cultivate your spiritual self.

Gate A gate may represent a portal from one state of being to another. Is there a gatekeeper? Do you meet the gatekeeper's criteria for passage to the next level? (see Door.)

Ghost An apparition or ghost appearing in a dream may suggest that something in your life is elusive or out of reach. If a person who has died appears in a dream, consider your past relationship to that person and what that individual symbolized in your life. A ghost of a living relative or friend in a dream may symbolize that you are in danger from someone you know, or if that ghost appears haggard it may symbolize an early death or a breaking off of a friendship.

Glass Glass is suggestive of separation and passive observation. Looking through glass in a dream may symbolize bitter disappointment clouding your brightest hopes. Receiving cut glass in a dream may suggest a reward for your efforts.

Gold Dreaming of gold jewelry or coins or a gold object indicates that success is forthcoming.

Goose A goose is often associated with a golden egg so that dreaming of one is a symbol of abundance. On the other hand, a goose in the oven or on fire suggests "your goose is cooked." Alternately, a "big goose egg" can mean zero or nothing.

Grave Like many dream symbols, a grave is one that grabs your attention, especially if it's your grave. A grave may portend a death, but not necessarily a physical one. It may mean that you're leaving the old behind, moving on to something new. As a

metaphor, a grave suggests that you may be dealing with a grave matter.

Green When green is a dominant color in a dream, it can be interpreted symbolically, like any object in a dream. Green is a color of healing, of growth, of money, and of new beginnings. It suggests positive movement in a matter at hand.

Gun A gun in your possession can symbolize protection, but it is also a phallic symbol and a sign of aggressive male behavior. If you shoot yourself, the act is what's important, not the gun. (see Suicide.)

H

Hail To dream of being in a hailstorm, or to hear hail knocking against the house represents being besieged by a troubling matter, thoughts, or emotions. However, if you dream of watching hail fall through sunshine and rain, it may suggest that fortune and pleasure will shine on you after a brief period of trouble or misery.

Hair Hair can appear in many different ways and is open to many interpretations. To dream that you have a beautiful head of hair and are combing it indicates thoughts of appearance over substance. To see your hair turn unexpectedly white suggests sudden misfortune and grief over a situation at hand, while a dream that you have a full head of

Zebras, Leopards

Dreaming of zebras running fast on the hoof indicates you are interested in fleeting enterprises. If you dream of a zebra wild in its native environment, you might pursue a fancy that could bring unsatisfactory results. Beware of those with multi-colored stripes!

If you dream of a leopard attacking you, your future success may encounter many difficulties. But if you kill the leopard, you will be victorious in life. If you dream of a caged leopard, it means that although your enemies surround you, they will fail to injure you.

white hair suggests a pleasing and fortunate passage through life. For a man to dream that his hair is thinning suggests misfortune due to generosity, or illness through worry. To see yourself covered in hair represents an indulgence in vice, while a dream of tangled and unkempt hair suggests trouble or concern over a matter at hand. For a woman to compare a white hair with a black one taken from her head symbolizes a hesitation between two paths.

Hammer A hammer may suggest strength or power. However, because it can be used for either constructive or destructive purposes, how the hammer is used is the key to its meaning.

Hand A dream of a hand (or hands) is open to numerous interpretations, depending on what the hand (or hands) is doing and the surrounding circumstances. Shaking hands is an act of friendship or an agreement. Hands folded in prayer may suggest you are seeking help or pursuing religious or spiritual urgings. A hand that is grasping at something may suggest a fear of death. As a metaphor, a hand may suggest that something important is "at hand." To see beautiful hands in a dream signifies feelings of great honor and rapid advancement in a matter at hand. Ugly and malformed hands point to disappointment and poverty. A detached hand represents solitude; people may fail to understand your views and feeling in a matter. Burning your hands in a dream suggests that you have overreached your abilities

and will suffer some loss because of it. A dream of washing your hands indicates participation in some joyous affair.

Harvest A harvest represents completion and abundance, and may indicate that your reward is due. As with all symbols, personal connotations are important. For instance, if you grew up on a farm, the dream could mean a longing to return to the past or to simpler times.

Hat A hat covers the head and can suggest that the person wearing it is concealing something, as in "keep it under your hat." Dreaming that you have a feather in your hat indicates achievement.

Hawk A hawk is a creature with keen sight. A soaring hawk in a dream might suggest the need for insight. It also might mean that the dreamer should keep a "hawk's eye" on someone or a situation.

Head Dreaming of a human head could indicate that you are ahead, or successful, on a matter of importance. A head also symbolizes a source of wisdom.

Heart To see a heart might relate to romantic inclinations. Is there a "heart throb" in your life? Alternately, the image might suggest you get to the "heart of the matter." On the negative side, if your heart is bleeding, it may mean that excessive sympathy is becoming a burden for you or the recipient, or both.

Heel The heel of your foot or shoe may symbolize vulnerability, as in the Achilles' heel story. It might also stand for an oppressive situation, as in "under someone's heel." Are you dealing with someone who is not trustworthy? He or she could be the heel in question.

Helmet Wearing a helmet in a dream denotes protection. The helmet could also symbolize that you need to guard your time, thoughts, or ideas.

High Tide To dream of a high tide symbolizes that a change, usually favorable, is in order, as in the phrase the "tides are turning."

Hogs A fat hog in a dream may suggest abundance, while a lean, hungry hog may foretell a troubling situation. If you grew up on a farm with hogs, the dream could relate to some aspect of your childhood. If the hogs are wallowing in mud, the indication might be that you've lowered your standards regarding a matter, or that you are groveling. The dream could also be a warning of such possibilities. A squealing hog suggests that something distasteful has occurred or will soon occur.

Horse A horse symbolizes strength, power, endurance, majesty, and virility. A man dreaming of a horse might desire virility and sexual prowess; a woman might be expressing a desire for sexual intercourse. Riding a horse suggests one is in a powerful position. White horses represent purity, while black horses represent a postponement of pleasure.

Hospital Finding oneself in a hospital suggests a need for healing, or a concern about one's health. Seeing someone else in a hospital might indicate that person is in a weakened condition. If you work in a hospital, the meaning of the dream may relate to work matters. In the latter case, other circumstances in the dream should be examined.

House Houses are common forums for dreams and may be of little consequence unless the house itself is the focus of the dream. If so, examine the type of house and its size. Discovering new rooms in a house or following secret passages in an old house can relate to an exploration of the unconscious. A small house might suggest a feeling of confinement. If a house is under construction, it could symbolize growth. If it's dilapidated, it suggests improvements are needed in some part of the dreamer's life.

Hugging To dream of your hugging a stranger suggests that you crave affection. If you know the person you are hugging, the interpretation will depend on your relationship to that person.

Humidity Dreaming of humidity represents the presence of an oppressive situation, either in work or at home.

Hurricane   Destructive and unpredictable, hurricane dreams can suggest different meanings depending on their context in the dream. To hear and see a hurricane coming at you symbolizes a feeling of torture and suspense over a matter at hand in which you are trying to avert failure. To dream of looking at the debris of a hurricane suggests that you will come close to calamity, but will be saved by the efforts of others. A dream in which you are in a house that is shattered by a hurricane and you are trying to save someone caught in the rubble may represent that your life will suffer many changes but that there is still no peace in domestic or business matters. To see people dead and wounded suggests that you are concerned over the troubles of others.

I

Ice   Ice may symbolize an emotional state of the dreamer or a person in the dream. Are you receiving an "icy reception?" If you are in a tenuous situation, you could be "skating on thin ice." In a sexual context, ice is frigidity. To dream of ice floating in a clear stream signifies an interruption of happiness, while dreaming of eating ice portends sickness.

Ice cream   A dream of ice cream, especially melting ice cream, may suggest that obstacles are being removed and that there is reason to celebrate. If ice cream is your favorite dessert, then the dream suggests that you're being rewarded or have reason to treat yourself. It can also stand for a desire for sexual fulfillment.

Icicles   Icicles represent danger or your concern over a matter that is hanging over you in some way. To dream of icicles falling off of trees or the eaves of a house may suggest that some misfortune will soon disappear. To dream of icicles on evergreens symbolizes that a bright future may be overshadowed by doubt.

Illness   If you dream of being ill, ask yourself if you're in need of being cared for and pampered. This dream might also be a message to watch your health.

Incest   A dream of a sexual encounter with someone within your family is not necessarily a warning about incest. Examine your relationship with the person in question. If there have been arguments or you're alienated from this family member, the dream may be your inner self expressing your love in a shocking way that will catch your attention.

Infants   Seeing infants in a dream suggests that pleasant surprises are near. Seeing an infant swimming represents a fortunate escape from some endeavor.

Initiation   Initiation suggests that a new path is opening for you. It could be a career change or advancement. Often, initiatory dreams relate to a spiritual quest.

Insects What's annoying or "bugging you"? If you dream of ants, you may be feeling "antsy" about a matter. (see Ant.)

Interview Being interviewed in a dream is similar to taking an examination. It suggests you're being judged. If you're surprised by the interview, it may indicate that you are feeling unprepared.

Invalid A dream of an invalid may indicate that you (or someone else) feel weak or incapable of living independently.

Island An island can be viewed as an exotic place or as a separate, isolated land. Dreaming of an island might mean that a vacation is due, especially if "going to the islands" is a vacation destination. Alternately, finding yourself on an "desert island" may suggest you are cut off from others or from your inner self.

J

Jail A jail may indicate that you're feeling restricted or confined and fear being punished. Or you may believe that you *should* be punished. Dreaming of being a jailer suggests the desire to control others or to gain more control of your own life.

January To dream of this month may mean that you will be associated with unloved companions or children.

Jaws Do you feel like you're under attack? Jaws can be the entry point to an archetypal journey into the underworld. Such a dream might also relate to a disagreement.

Jewelry In a material sense, jewelry can symbolize affluence, but look to other aspects of the dream for confirmation. Jewelry can also stand for inner wealth, psychic protection, or healing.

Job Dreaming that you are at work on the job may indicate that you're overworked, you're deeply focused on some aspect of your job, or you desire to work harder and achieve more.

Judge If you're the judge, the dream suggests that you have a choice to make. A judge can also represent justice or fairness. Alternately, a judge may stand for a part of you that criticizes your impulsive behavior. Or perhaps you're concerned that you're being judged. Who is judging you?

July A dream that takes place in this month symbolizes a depressed outlook that will suddenly change to unimagined pleasure and good fortune.

Jumping Pick your metaphor: Are you "a jump ahead," "jumping to conclusions," "jumping the gun," or "jumping for joy"? A series of jumps may be the take-off point for a flying dream. A great leap can also symbolize success or achievement or "a leap of faith."

June For a dream to take place in June symbolizes unusual gains in all undertakings. For a woman to dream of vegetation, dying, or a drought suggests a lasting sorrow and loss.

Jungle A jungle may represent a hidden, dark part of the self that you've been avoiding. Your unconscious might be telling you of a need to explore this part of yourself. It may also represent a great, untapped fertility within you for spiritual growth.

Junk If you dream of junk or clutter, ask yourself if you're clinging to the past, to things or ideas that are no longer useful. If something you value appears as junk in a dream, it may indicate that you need to reassess your values.

K

Kangaroo To see a kangaroo might suggest the dreamer is "hopping mad" about something. It could also mean that you have the ability to "hop to" a particular matter that is pending.

Key A key can stand for a part of yourself that you've locked away, or something that you can now access if you have the key. Such a dream may also indicate you hold the key to your own concerns.

Killing A dream of killing someone is probably not a warning that you might turn into a killer. Instead, the meaning is more likely a symbolic act of aggression. Who did you kill and how is that person involved in your life? If you don't recognize the person, the dream may symbolize killing off an unwanted part of yourself.

King A king is a ruler and a powerful authority figure. Dreaming of a king may mean you are seeking status or support. The king may represent your father or some other powerful figure in your life. If you're the king, the indication is that you have achieved a high level of authority or are a highly capable individual.

Kiss A kiss suggests a romantic involvement, but can also be a metaphor as in "kiss and make up," or the "kiss of death." In the former, the dream kiss might indicate a reconciliation is as hand. A kiss of death spells the end to something, such as a way of life. For married people to kiss each other symbolizes harmony in the home life. Is it dark or light out during the kiss? The former suggests danger or an illicit situation while the latter represents honorable intentions. To dream of kissing someone on the neck symbolizes a passionate inclination in a matter at hand.

Kitchen Going to a kitchen in a dream suggests some part of your life is in need of nourishment. Alternately, a kitchen might suggest that something is in the process of being "cooked up," like a new project. Note what you're doing in the kitchen.

Kitten To discover kittens in a closet or a basement suggests the awakening of hidden aspects of the self. It can also relate to new ideas and projects.

Knife A knife is a symbol of aggression and the male sexual organ. Examine the other aspects of the dream. Are you being stabbed in the back? Do you hold the knife or is someone threatening you with it? A rusty knife may symbolize dissatisfaction, a sharp knife worry, and a broken knife defeat.

Knight A knight signifies honor and high standing. Are you searching for a knight or are you acting like a knight? Knights are also armored and stand for protection.

Knob A knob appearing in a dream may imply a need to get a handle on a matter. Knobs also signify a means of passing from one room to the next, or one way of life to another.

Knot Dreaming of knots suggests that you're all tied up about something—that worries and anxieties are troubling you. You may feel as if you're "tied in a knot." Alternately, if you or someone close to you is "tying the knot," the dream might signify a concern about an upcoming marriage.

L

Laboratory A laboratory is a place where experiments are conducted. The implication is that the dreamer is unsatisfied with a present situation and experimenting with something new. The dreamer might also be testing a relationship with someone.

Labyrinth A dream of a labyrinth may indicate that you feel trapped in a situation or a relationship and are looking for a way out. It may also refer to the intricacies of a spiritual journey.

Ladder Are you going up or climbing down the ladder? An ascent may symbolize a higher step into an inner realm or a promotion to a higher status in one's career or other pursuits.

Lagoon Lagoons symbolize doubt and confusion over an emotional matter or a stagnant situation.

Lake In the Freudian interpretation, a lake is symbolic of the vagina. In the Jungian world, lakes and other bodies of water stand for the unconscious or emotions. In one interpretation, the dreamer who dives into a lake is returning to the womb. In the other, the dreamer explores the unconscious. But if neither interpretation fits, examine the other elements in the dream. Is the lake clear or muddy? The former suggests lucidity and strength of purpose, while the latter may

Ivy & Mistletoe

Dreaming of ivy growing on trees or a house indicates you will have excellent health and success. Many joys in your life could follow this dream. For a young woman to dream of ivy clinging to a wall in moonlight portends she will have a secret affair with a young man. Beware of dreaming of withered ivy. It indicates broken engagements and sadness.

To dream of mistletoe signifies great happiness and honor is to come your way. If you are young and dream of mistletoe, it indicates you will have many pleasant times in your future.

represent muddled feelings and an unsure direction in a matter at hand.

Lamb A lamb may stand for gentleness or vulnerability, as in "a lamb to the slaughter," or it may be a spiritual symbol as in "sacrificial lamb" and "lamb of God." However, a dream of a lamb may simply symbolize a general love of animals.

Lamp A lamp, like a lantern, represents light or illumination and suggests the dreamer is searching for truth.

Lap A symbol of security, such as "the lap of luxury," to dream of sitting on someone's lap signifies safety from some troubling situation. A dream of a cat in a lap represents danger from a seductive enemy.

Law suits Dreams of legal matters suggest the dreamer is being judged.

Leeches Leeches are nightmarish creatures that suck blood. Is there someone in your life who is draining you of energy?

Legs Legs in various states of health and appearance are frequently seen in dreams and open to many interpretations depending on the context. To dream of admiring well-shaped legs suggests a loss of judgment; to see misshapen legs represents unsuccessful endeavors and ill-tempered friends. A wooden leg represents deception to friends, while a wounded leg suggests a loss of power and standing. A dream of ulcers on your legs suggests a drain on your resources to help others. A young woman who admires her own legs indicates vanity, and if she has hairy legs then it may indicate feelings of dominanation over her mate. Dreaming that your own legs are clean and well shaped represents a happy future with faithful friends.

Letter A letter sometimes symbolizes a message from your unconscious to you. If you're unable to read the letter, look at other aspects of the dream for clues. An anonymous letter may signify an injurious concern from an unspecified source. Blue ink symbolizes steadfastness and affection, red ink may suggest suspicion and jealousy, and a letter with a black border may represent distress and death of some kind. Receiving a letter written on black paper with white ink may suggest feelings of misery and disappointment over a matter. If this letter passed between husband and wife or lovers, then concerns over the relationship may be present. A torn letter may suggest concerns that hopeless mistakes may ruin your reputation.

Lightning A dream of lightning indicates a flash of inspiration or sudden awareness about the truth of a matter. Lightning can also mean a purging or purification, or fear of authority or death.

Lion To dream of a lion signifies that you are driven by a great force. Subduing a lion indicates victory in a matter. If you are overtaken by the lion, the dream suggests that you may be vulnerable to an attack of some sort. A caged lion may mean that you will succeed as long as the opposition is held in check.

Lottery To dream of a lottery signifies chance or throwing your fate to luck. If you dream of holding the winning number, then luck and good fortune in a matter at hand may follow. To see others winning in a lottery may suggest that many friends will be brought together in a pleasing manner. A young woman dreaming of a lottery may indicate a reckless attitude.

Luggage Luggage stands for your personal effects or what you carry with you on a journey. What happens to the luggage? Lost luggage might be a concern about your identity or about being prepared for the journey. Stolen luggage might suggest that you feel someone is interfering with your attempt to reach a goal.

M

Magic This could point to the magical aspects of creativity or, on the darker side, to deceit and trickery.

Man To dream of a handsome man, some individual you do not know, represents an enjoyment of life. If the man is disfigured, then perplexities and sorrow may involve you in a matter at hand. For a woman to dream of a handsome man can suggest that distinction will be offered.

Manuscript A manuscript represents the collection of your hopes and desires. To interpret the dream, note the shape or appearance of the manuscript. Is it finished or unfinished? Are you at work on it? Did you lose it?

Map You're searching for a new path to follow or are being guided in a new direction.

March A dream that occurs in this month may symbolize unsatisfactory results in a business matter.

Mask Masks hide our appearances and our feelings from others, but the dream may signify that you are hiding your emotions on a particular matter from yourself. If others are wearing masks, then perhaps you are confronted with a situation in which you think someone is not being truthful.

May A dream of May indicates fortunate times and pleasures for the young. To dream of a freakish appearance of nature suggests sudden sorrow and misery.

Medicine Taking medicine in a dream can be a potent symbol of healing your "wounds." It also suggests that you have "to take your medicine," do what is necessary or required of you.

Merry-go-round A merry-go-round suggests that you are going round and round in life and not moving ahead. The same would apply to someone else you dream of on a merry-go-round.

Meteor A meteor or falling star may symbolize that your wish will come true, or it could suggest that you are engaged in wishful thinking. Look at the other elements in the dream and decide which possibility is true for you.

Microphone A microphone may symbolize the desire to draw attention to yourself, or to gain power over others. Alternately, a microphone may suggest a concern that you are not forceful enough, and need help in projecting yourself.

Microscope A microscope symbolizes the need or wish to find something that's out of sight or hidden from you.

Milk Milk symbolizes nurturing. It can also represent strength and virility.

Mist Like fog, mist indicates a period of temporary uncertainty. Seeing others in a mist may mean that you will profit by their misfortune and uncertainty.

Money Money represents energy, power, and influence. Dreaming of gaining money suggests abundance; losing sums of money symbolizes a draining of energy, power, and influence. To dream of stealing money suggests danger.

Morning Morning represents a fresh start, or a sudden change of fortune for the positive. To dream of a cloudy morning indicates that heavy matters may overwhelm you.

Mother To see your mother symbolizes pleasing results from any endeavor. What is the context in which she appears? To converse with her suggests you may soon receive good news. To hear your mother calling represents that you are in need of a correction in your life.

Mother-in-Law A dream in which your mother-in-law appears suggests that a pleasant reconciliation is in order over a matter after some serious disagreement.

Mountain A mountain represents a challenge. If you're climbing the mountain, you're working to achieve your goals. Descending a mountain suggests that things are easier now; your success may have ensured your future.

Mule Mules are known for their contrary behavior, as in "stubborn as a mule." To dream of a mule suggests that the dreamer may be acting in a stubborn manner that others find annoying. Mules also are work animals. Consider whether you are rebelling against some aspect of your job or career.

Murder Murder symbolizes repressed anger either at yourself or others. If you murder someone you know, consider your relationship with that person. If you're the one murdered, then the dream may symbolize a personal transformation.

Music Music in a dream symbolizes emotional matters. Consider the type of music you heard and how you related to it. Did it fill you with joy? Did it make you sad or angry?

N

Nail A nail in a dream can have a variety of meanings. To "nail it down" suggests putting something together or holding it together. If you "hit the nail on the head,"

Naked/Nudity Being nude in a dream can symbolize a wish for exposure, to be seen or heard. It can also relate to a need to bare the truth. Alternately, a dream of nudity can be sexually related and suggests that the dreamer is no longer inhibited. To dream of swimming naked may represent an

illicit affair that will end badly, or that you have many admirers.

Neck A neck can be a sexual symbol related to the slang term *necking*. A neck can also represent taking a chance, as in "sticking one's neck out." Alternately, if there is pain related to this part of the body, something might be giving you a "pain in the neck."

Needle A dream of a needle and thread might indicate that a matter is being sewn up, or a deal is being completed. A needle might also suggest that someone is needling you. To dream of threading a needle symbolizes that you may be burdened with caring for others, to look for a needle augurs useless worries. To break a needle in a dream signifies loneliness and poverty.

Nest A nest is a symbol of home and might relate to the desire to return home. If you are moving, it might relate to your concerns about your new home. If there is an egg in the nest, the dream might relate to a concern about your savings or "nest egg."

Night A night setting for a dream might suggest something is hidden or obscured. There might be a need to illuminate something. Being surrounded by night in a dream suggests oppression and hardship.

Nose A nose can be a symbol of intrusive behavior, as in "sticking one's nose into someone else's business." Dreaming of a

PASTURE, FIELDS, GRASS

To dream of green fields, ripe with corn or grain, indicates you will have great abundance. If you dream of plowed fields, you will have wealth and prestige at a young age. Of course if you dream of a field full of dead corn, expect a dreary future.

If you dream of a pasture freshly plowed and ready for planting, a long struggle will soon be resolved and you will have great success.

To dream of green grass signifies good things will happen in your life. If you are in business, you will soon be wealthy. If you are an artist, you soon will become well-known. If you are about to marry, you will have a safe, happy life with your partner.

nose may suggest that someone is interfering in your life or that you are being nosy.

November November dreams usually suggest a season of indifferent success in all affairs.

Nurse A dream of a nurse suggests that you are being healed or are in need of healing. It also implies a desire to be pampered or nursed. The dream could also relate to a relationship or a project that you are nursing along.

Nursing A dream of nursing could indicate an idea or situation that needs nurturing.

O

Oak An oak tree represents strength, stability, endurance, truth, and wisdom. A dream with an oak may suggest that a strong, proper foundation has been established in a matter.

Oar An oar can represent masculinity and strength; it dips into the water, the emotions. To row vigorously suggests a need for aggressiveness or that you are moving through an issue. If you have only one oar and are rowing in a circle, it might suggest frustration at the lack of forward movement.

Oasis An oasis suggests that you've arrived at a place of sustenance, that you

are being nurtured. Or it might suggest that you're taking a break from your journey or have succeeded in reaching one destination on the journey. Alternately, the dream might imply that you need a vacation, a break.

Ocean A dream of the ocean often represents the emotional setting of your life. The context of the dream is important here. Sailing through rough seas suggests you are capable of dealing with life's ups and downs. Large waves can also represent untapped powers of the unconscious. Fishing in the ocean and catching something big can suggest an opportunity is at hand or that you are delving into the wealth of your unconscious. To be lost at sea may suggest you have lost your moorings, that you are adrift in life and in need of direction. To be anchored in the ocean may indicate you have found a place in life.

October To dream of October portends success. New friendships or business affairs will ripen into lasting relationships.

Officer An officer, whether military, police, or corporate, represents an authority figure. Dreaming of an officer, especially if you don't know the person, can suggest a fear or wariness of authority figures or a need for guidance from a person with authority.

Oil A dream of oil represents great wealth or inner wealth, as in a dream of pumping crude oil to the surface. Using

aromatic oils in a dream can represent sacred matters. A person associated with oil might be slick, or a smooth-talker.

Old man If the old man guides or directs you in some way, he is, in Jungian thought, an archetypal figure. If the man appears to be weak or injured in some way, he could symbolize some part of yourself that needs attention or someone in your life who needs your help. It may also mean that you need to redefine your beliefs about aging.

Old woman In Jungian terms, an old woman is an archetypal symbol of the power of the feminine, or the gatekeeper between life and death. If she is weak or injured, she may represent a part of yourself that needs attention or someone in your life who needs your help.

Oven An oven might represent a gestation period. It also symbolizes the womb and feminine energy. A dream of an oven could relate to a pregnancy.

Owl An owl represents both wisdom and mystery and is a symbol of the unconscious.

Ox To dream of an ox implies great strength and endurance and an ability to carry on against great odds.

P

Painting If a wall is being painted, the act may suggest that something is being hidden or covered up. Painting at an easel may indicate artistic or creative talents are ready to be expressed.

Park Dreaming of a park may suggest a wish to relax and enjoy life. Walking in an unlit park at night may mean that you are delving into areas of darkness and danger, or that you are dealing with hidden or mysterious matters.

Party To find yourself at a party in a dream suggests that a celebration is in order. If you are concerned about a particular matter that remains unsettled, the dream may indicate a favorable resolution.

Peacock A dream of a peacock suggests that you have something to show off, a reason to be proud, similar to the peacock that displays its colorful tail feathers.

Photograph Since a photograph is an image of a person or object rather than the real thing, a dream of a photograph hints of deception. If you recognize a person in a dream photo, be careful in your dealings with the person and look for hidden meaning in the person's actions. To dream of having your own photograph made suggests that you may unwittingly be the cause of your own troubles.

Physician A physician appearing in a dream might indicate that a healing is at hand. A physician is also an authority figure who might be offering a diagnosis on some matter. Sometimes, a physician may take the form of a trusted friend who isn't a doctor but whose nurturing traits are healing.

Piano Music in general represents joyous or festive feelings. Note the condition and type of music coming from the piano. A broken piano symbolizes displeasure in your achievements; an old-fashioned piano suggests neglect over a matter at hand.

Pill Taking a pill in a dream suggests that the dreamer may be required to go along with something unpleasant. But positive results should follow.

Pilot A pilot symbolizes someone soaring high and in control in spite of the fast pace. A dream of a pilot may represent that you're in the pilot's seat concerning some issue in your life.

Planet Seeing a planet or visiting another planet in a dream may indicate a new adventure, a new way of thinking, or a new dimension of creativity.

Polar Bear These creatures may represent that trickery or deceit is upon you. Maybe one of your enemies will appear as a friend to overcome you. However, seeing the skin of a polar bear suggests that you will successfully triumph over adversity.

Police Police officers represent authority; they uphold the law. A dream of police may serve as a warning against breaking the law or bending rules. It might suggest a fear of punishment. Alternately, the dream may indicate a desire for justice and to punish the wrongdoers in a matter of concern.

Pond A pond signifies tranquility and a placid outlook in either the dreamer or a person in the dream.

Pregnant If a woman dreams of being pregnant, it could indicate a desire for a child or the onset of the condition. A pregnancy could also symbolize something new coming into being in the dreamer's life, an idea or project that is gestating.

Priest A priest represents a benign spiritual authority who serves as a guide. Alternately, a priest might symbolize a

dictatorial figure or one who judges and condemns. A dream of a priest may indicate the need to follow or eschew conventional religion. Look to surrounding details for clarification.

Prison Constraint and restriction are implied. If you see yourself at work in a prison, the dream might suggest that you've limited your creativity or that you feel it's difficult to "escape" your job for a better one.

Professor A professor may represent knowledge, wisdom, and higher education.

Prophet A prophet provides knowledge, guidance, and perhaps a peek at the future. Or, the symbol may indicate that you're in need of guidance.

Puddle Stepping into or stomping through puddles represents a parting or clearing away of troubles, with good times to follow. To dream that you are just wetting your feet in a puddle may mean that trouble will follow a pleasurable experience.

Pump To see a pump in a dream denotes that energy is available to meet your needs. A functioning pump could also symbolize good health. A broken pump signifies a breakdown or disruption of the usual way of doing things.

Puppet A dream of a puppet might indicate that you are feeling manipulated in

some aspect of your life. Alternately, if you are behind the puppet, the dream may indicate that you're acting in a manipulative manner.

Q

Quarrel A dream of a quarrel may indicate that an inner turmoil is plaguing you. If the person you're quarreling with is identifiable, look at your relationship with the person and see if you can identify the area of disagreement. There could be clues in the dream that indicate a way to resolve the differences.

Queen Both an authority and a mother figure, the queen is an archetypal symbol of power. If you are the queen, the dream may be suggesting a desire for leadership. If someone else is the queen, the dream may indicate that you see the woman as capable and powerful.

Quest A dream of a quest may indicate a desire to achieve a goal or embark on an adventure.

Quicksand A dream of quicksand indicates that you need to watch where you are headed. If you're already in the quicksand, then you're probably mired in an emotional matter and feel as if you can't escape. It could refer to either business or personal matters.

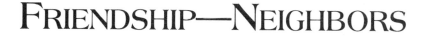

FRIENDSHIP—NEIGHBORS

I f you dream of a gathering of your friends and they are all happy, you will have a pleasant event to attend soon. If you dream of a gathering of your friends and they are sad and gloomy— call them; something is probably amiss.

If you dream of a neighbor, be prepared to spend hours ironing out problems due to unwarranted gossip. If you dream your neighbor is sad—watch out. You might quarrel with that neighbor.

Quilt A quilt suggests warmth and protection. A patchwork quilt symbolizes the sewing together of various aspects of your life to form a protective covering.

R

Rabbit The rabbit is a symbol of fertility and magic, as the rabbit pulled from the magician's hat. Although fertility could relate to the conception of children, it might also concern financial abundance, the success of a particular project, or other matters. A white rabbit may signify faithfulness in love.

Race If you are racing in a dream, then perhaps you're involved in an overly competitive situation or you're in a rush. The message might be that it's time to slow down and relax.

Rain A fresh downpour symbolizes a washing or cleansing away of the old. Alternately, a rainy day may indicate a gloomy situation. To hear the patter of rain on the roof may signify domestic bliss, while seeing a downpour of rain from inside a house may represent requited love and fortune. Seeing it rain on others may mean that you are excluding friends from your confidence.

Rainbow Usually seen after rain storms in nature, their appearance in dreams may represent that favorable conditions will arise after a brief period of unpleasantness. Seeing a low-hanging rainbow over verdant trees may signify success in any endeavor.

Rams If you dream of a ram charging you with its head down, that indicates you are under attack from some quarter. If the ram is near, it may indicate that the attack is near or that you will have little time to react. A ram charging from a distance suggests that you will have time to respond to the situation. Consider whether someone in your life is trying to "ram" something down your throat. If the ram is quietly grazing in a pasture, the indication could be that you have powerful allies on your side.

Rapids Rapids represent danger and a fear of being swept away by emotions.

Rat Rats are generally associated with filth and dilapidation. Dreaming of a rat or rats may suggest the deterioration of a situation. Ask yourself who the "rat" is in your life.

Red The color red is often associated with vitality and energy, the heart, and blood. The color red in a dream can also mean anger or strong emotions as in "seeing red." Red often indicates that the dream originates from the deepest level of your being.

Referee A referee in a dream can symbolize an inner battle taking place or it can relate to conflict in your daily life. Can you identify the issue? If so, weigh the two sides, negotiate, and reach a settlement.

Sometimes working with a third party, not involved in the dispute, can help.

Rice Rice is the dietary staple of the majority of the world's population. To dream of rice is a symbol of fertility and good fortune.

River A dream of floating down a river might indicate a lack of motivation. Are you allowing surrounding circumstances to direct your life, rather than taking charge? A dream of a surging, frothing river may relate to deep-seated anger. In mythology, a river sometimes relates to death or the passing from one state to another.

Road A road is a means of getting from one place to another. What is the condition of the road in your dream? A smooth and straight road suggests the path ahead is easy. A road with dips and curves may indicate that you need to be aware, flexible, and ready for change. A roadblock suggests that there are detours in your path.

Rose A rose symbolizes the feminine and is associated with romance, beauty, and love. A dream of someone handing you a rose may indicate an offering of love. A rose can also relate to good and evil. If someone crushes a rose, that person's intent might be evil.

Ruins To dream of something in ruins suggests the deterioration of some condition in your life. Keep in mind that when things fall apart an opportunity to rebuild inevitably appears. If you are planning a trip, especially one to another culture, a dream of ancient ruins could symbolize the adventure of the journey ahead. Alternately, it could signify that you have the ability to access knowledge or wisdom from the past.

Running When you run in a dream, it might be either toward or away from something; you may be in a hurry to escape from something or to reach a goal. Depending on the circumstances, the dream may indicate that you need to hurry, or that you're rushing around too much and need to rest. Are you running alone or with others? The former may symbolize that you will overcome your competition in business matters, while the latter may represent your participation in a joyous occasion.

S

Sacrifice To see yourself sacrificed in a dream suggests that you're giving up something important for the sake of others. Closely examine your feelings about the matter. Decide what changes, if any, need to be made.

Sailor A dream of a sailor suggests that you are working on a ship. Symbolically, it could mean that you are working on matters dealing with the unconscious or emotions. (see Ship and Water.)

Saint A saint in a dream indicates you're being guided or are seeking guidance from a higher source.

School A school dream may indicate that you are gaining knowledge at a deep level of your existence or that what you are learning in your waking life is being processed and adapted by the unconscious. What happens in the school is important in the interpretation. If you're late to class or show up to take a test without ever having gone to class, the dream is a common symbol for feeling unprepared for something in your life. If you're looking for a school or classroom, the dream may be telling you that expanding your education is in order.

Scissors Is there something in your life you want to cut off? Scissors also indicate a need to "cut it out." The person with the scissors may be acting "snippy."

Scrapbook Scrapbooks are full of things from the past that are filed away and forgotten. Note the other details of the dream. Are you viewing a scrapbook with someone? What are you placing in the scrapbook? It may suggest that you have an unpleasant situation that needs to be put in the past.

Sea Dreams of the sea represent unfulfilled longings or unchanging emotions.

September Dreaming of September represents good luck and fortune.

Shadow Dreaming of your shadow may suggest that you need to address hidden parts of yourself. Perhaps you do not accept these darker aspects of your personality and project them onto others. The dream may also suggest that you need to incorporate the shadow side into your psyche.

Shaking Hands The handshake marks either a new beginning or an ending to a situation. Are you saying farewell to someone in a dream? Then perhaps you are saying goodbye to a matter at hand. To dream of shaking hands with a prominent leader may mean you will be held in esteem by strangers in a new situation.

Shaving Is there something in your life that needs cleaning up or removed? To dream of shaving yourself connotes that you are in charge of your future. Shaving with a dull razor suggests a troublesome or painful issue. A clean shaven countenance suggests a smooth journey through a matter at hand.

Sheep Do you perceive yourself as one of a flock? This can be a comforting image in terms of being part of a community. Or it may indicate that you lack individuality or the will to strike out on your own.

Shell A shell usually symbolizes a womb. Depending on the circumstances of the dream, it can portend a birth of a child or a new project. A shell can also symbolize protection.

Ship Since a ship travels on water, the dream may signify a voyage through the unconscious or a journey involving your emotions. The state of the ship and the condition of the water should be considered in the interpretation. To see a ship in a storm may indicate your concern over a tempestuous or unfortunate affair, either in business or personal matters. To dream of others shipwrecked may symbolize a feeling of inadequacy in protecting friends or family.

Shoes Shoes are a means of moving ahead. Shiny, new shoes might suggest a journey is about to begin. Well-worn shoes, on the other hand, might indicate that one is weary of the journey or that it is near completion. Mismatched shoes might indicate that the journey is multifaceted. Consider the old cliche: "If the shoe fits, wear it."

Shovel A tool for digging, a shovel in a dream may indicate that you are searching for something or are about to embark on a quest for inner knowledge. A shovel might also represent labor or hard work ahead. A broken shovel could mean that you are experiencing frustration in your work.

Shower To dream of taking a shower may symbolize a spiritual renewal. It might also signify a bonus or reward showered upon the dreamer.

Sickness/ Illness If you dream of being ill, ask yourself if you're in need of being cared for and pampered. This dream might also be a message to watch your health. To dream of a family member who is sick represents some misfortune or issue that is troubling your domestic life.

Singing Hearing singing in a dream signifies a pleasant and cheerful attitude and that you may hear promising news over a matter at hand. If you are singing in the dream, note the type (happy, sad) of song you are singing.

Skating Dreaming of skating may signify to the dreamer that they are gliding over a matter at hand, or that they may be skating on thin ice. Note all the aspects of the dream.

Skull To dream of a skull and crossbones is a traditional sign of danger and possibly death—a warning.

Sky Dreaming of the sky symbolizes hope, vitality, and a creative force.

Smoke If you dream of smoke filling a room, it suggests that a matter at hand is being obscured. On the other hand, if the smoke is clearing, clarity is imminent.

WIND, GALES

D reaming of wind softly blowing signifies you will receive a considerable inheritance from a beloved one. Although you experience sadness over the death of this loved one, you will know happiness in the future. If you dream you are walking against a brisk wind, it indicates you are courageous, resist temptations, and pursue your hopes with a plucky determination. You will be successful. If, however, in your dream the wind blows you along against your wishes, it signifies you might have disappointments in love and in business.

If, of all things, you dream you are caught in a gale, watch out—you might have business losses.

Snake A snake is an archetypal image that can have numerous interpretations. In mythology, snakes are symbols of wisdom, of healing and fertility, and—in the shedding of skin—of renewal. Snakes can also symbolize the dangers of the underworld. In Christianity, the snake symbolizes temptation and the source of evil. In some Eastern traditions, the snake is related to a power that rises from the base of the spine and can be a symbol of transformation. The Freudian interpretation relates snakes to the male genitalia. How you view snakes symbolically and other aspects of the dream should guide you in your interpretation.

Snow Snow can represent purity if seen in a pristine landscape. Since snow is a solidified form of water, it can also stand for frozen emotions. If the snow is melting, the suggestion is that frozen feelings are thawing. To find yourself in a snowstorm may represent uncertainty in an emotional matter, or sorrow in failing to enjoy some long expected pleasure. Dreaming of snow-capped mountains in the distance suggests that your ambitions will yield no advancement. Eating snow symbolizes a failure to realize ideals.

Spaceship A spaceship in a dream may suggest a journey into the unknown, or symbolize a spiritual quest.

Spear Thrusting a spear at someone in a dream may represent an effort to thrust your will on another person. If the spear is hurled over a field, toward a mountain, or an ocean, the dream may mean that you are making a powerful statement to the world.

Spider Spiders may symbolize a careful and energetic approach to your work and that you will be pleasantly rewarded for your labors. To dream of a spider spinning its web signifies that your homelife will be happy and secure, while many spiders represent good health and friends. A confrontation with a large spider may signify a quick ascent to fame and fortune, unless the large spider bites you, in which it may represent the loss of money or reputation.

Squirrel To see these friendly creatures may mean that pleasant acquaintances will soon visit, or that you will advance in business.

Stairs Climbing a stairway in a dream can mean that you are on your way to achieving a goal. Descending a stairs, or falling down one, might indicate a fall in prestige or economic status. To sit on a step could suggest that you are pausing in your everyday life with its challenges to consider where things stand.

Statue Dreaming of a statue or statues could signify a lack of movement in your life. Statues are also cold and can symbolize frozen feelings.

Stillborn To dream of a stillborn infant indicates a premature ending or some distressing circumstance in a matter at hand.

Stones Stones can represent small irritations or obstacles that must be overcome. Seeing yourself throw a stone in a dream may mean that you have cause to reprove someone.

Storm To dream of an approaching storm indicates emotional turmoil in some aspect of your life. Dark skies and thunder may also be a forewarning that danger is approaching. Alternately, a storm could symbolize rapid changes occurring in your life.

Suicide A dream of killing yourself probably is a symbolic reflection of what's going on in your conscious life. Such a dream might reflect a personal transformation, a divorce, changing careers, or other major life shifts. You are essentially killing your past, becoming a new person.

Sun Dreaming of the sun is usually fortuitous. The sun is the symbol of light, warmth, and energy. In Native American lore, the sun symbolizes the father or the masculine principal.

Swimming A dream of swimming suggests the dreamer is immersed in an exploration of emotional matters or the unconscious.

Sword A sword is a symbol of strength and power. It also can cut to the bone. Dreaming of a sword might suggest that aggressive action is required.

T

Table To dream of an empty table might suggest a concern about a lack or shortage of possessions, while a table covered with food may symbolize a time of abundance.

Tamborine The appearance of a tamborine symbolizes pleasure in some unusual undertaking about to take place.

Tattoo Tattoos are associated with the strange and exotic. To dream of seeing your body tattooed suggests that some difficulty will cause you to make a long absence from home or familiar surroundings. Dreaming that you are a tattooist suggests that your desire for some strange experience may alienate you from friends.

Teeth Teeth are what you use to bite. If you lose your bite, you lose power. Losing teeth might also symbolize a loss of face. It could also be a metaphor for "loose" or careless speech. Note the other aspects of the dream. For example, to examine your teeth suggests that you exercise caution in a matter at hand. To clean your teeth represents that some struggle is necessary to keep your standing. Admiring your teeth for their whiteness suggests that wishes for a pleasant occupation and happiness will be fulfilled. To dream that you pull your own teeth and are feeling around the cavity with your tongue signifies your trepidation over a situation about to be entered into. Dreaming of imperfect teeth is one of the worst dreams to have for it connotes bad feelings about your appearance and well-being.

Telephone A telephone might symbolize the attempt to contact the unconscious. If the phone is ringing and no one is answering, the dream might suggest that you are ignoring the call of your unconscious.

Tent A tent provides shelter and is usually associated with camping. A dream of a tent could indicate that you are in need of a getaway, a retreat from everyday life.

Thaw Thawing represents the rebirth or return to pleasant conditions. To dream of seeing ice thaw may symbolize that something or someone that was giving you trouble will soon yield pleasure and profit.

The President of the United States Not as uncommon as it may seem, to talk with the President of the United States in a dream may represent an interest in lofty ideals or political matters, or a strong desire to be a politician.

Thief If you dream of someone stealing something, the implication is that something is being taken from you. It could be a boss or colleague who is stealing your energy or ideas, rather than an actual theft of goods. If you're the thief, the message may be a warning that you are taking what you don't deserve and that you should change your ways.

Thirst A dream in which you are thirsty suggests that you are in need of nourishment, either physical, mental, or emotional. To see others relieving their thirst suggests that this nourishment may come from others.

Thorn A thorn may represent an annoyance of some sort, "a thorn in your side."

Tiger Aggressive and fierce in the wild, to see these animals in your dream may symbolize that you are under persecution or will be tormented. However, if you see yourself fending off an attack, this may mean that you will be extremely successful in all your ventures.

Tornado Swift and terrible agents of destruction in nature, a dream involving a tornado suggests that your desire for a quick resolution in a matter at hand may lead to disappointment.

Torrent To dream of a seething torrent of water suggests a profound unrest in the emotional state of the dreamer or a person in the dream.

Tower To dream of a tower could symbolize vigilance, as a watchtower, or punishment or isolation as a guard tower. Dreaming of being in an "ivory tower" indicates that you or the subject of your dream is out of touch with the everyday world.

Train A train symbolizes a journey. Look at the other elements in the dream to understand the nature of your journey. If the train isn't moving, the dream might be suggesting some impediment in your life. If you can't find your luggage, the dream might indicate that you are concerned that you're not ready for this journey. If you are on a smoothly running train, but there are no tracks, the dream might signify that you are concerned over some affair that will eventually be resolved satisfactorily. Traveling on the wrong train may indicate your journey is in need of a correction.

Treasure A dream of a treasure may suggests a hidden talent or hidden abilities that you can now unearth. It could indicate latent psychic abilities.

Tree A tree is a symbol of strength and foundation. It may also symbolize inner strength. A tree exists both below the earth and above it. In that sense, a tree transcends the sky above and the earth below and stands for the realms of nature and the spirit. To dream of a tree in new foliage represents a pleasant outcome to your hopes and desires. Tree-climbing dreams may signify a quick ascent in business. Green trees newly felled augur unexpected unhappiness after a period of prosperity and delight.

Trial A dream of being on trial suggests that you are being judged, or are afraid of being judged. Alternately, a trial in a dream could indicate that you are judging others too harshly.

Triplets To dream of triplets indicates success in a matter where failure was feared. For a man to dream of his wife having triplets represents a pleasing end to a situation that has long been in dispute. To hear newly born triplets crying suggests a disagreement that will soon be resolved in your favor.

Tunnel From a Freudian perspective, a dream of a tunnel suggests a vagina, and a train entering the tunnel represents sexual intercourse. A tunnel may also be a link between two conditions: When you exit the tunnel, you will enter a new state of mind.

Turtle While dreaming of a turtle might symbolize slow, painstaking movement, the shelled creature is also a symbol of spiritual development.

Twins A dream of twins may mean that there are two parts to a matter of concern or two aspects to your personality. Seeing twins in a dream symbolizes security in a business matter and faithfulness in a domestic issue.

BELLS

———■———

Dreaming of bells tolling means a distant friend will die. If you dream of a joyous bell ringing, however, expect success in all aspects of your life.

If you dream of an alarm ringing in warning, it indicates you have worries about some aspect of your life. If you dream you hear a doorbell ringing, expect to be called away to visit a friend or relative in need.

U

Umbrella An umbrella represents protection against adverse conditions or an emotional flood from the unconscious. If the umbrella is closed and you're being soaked by a downpour, the indication is that you are open to your emotional needs.

Underground To dream of being in an underground habitation often symbolizes contact with your subconscious. Other images in the dream will provide more meaning to the nature of the contact. Is there something you've been hiding here that should be brought to the "surface"? Ask yourself how you feel about the situation. Do you feel protected by the underground cavern or room? Or are you being held prisoner or hiding? Dreaming of an underground railway could indicate passage to another state of being, a personal transformation. Examine the event of your life to see how such an interpretation would fit. (see Basement.)

Underwear A dream of underwear may symbolize that you are exposing something that is under cover or hidden. It could indicate that you're bringing matters from the unconscious to the surface.

Unicycle If you are riding a unicycle in a dream, you may be concerned about balance. Alternately, you're the "big wheel" and on your own.

United States Mailbox A mailbox is a symbol of authority; consequently, putting a letter in a mailbox may mean you are submitting to authority, or feeling guilt over a particular matter.

Urination A dream in which you urinate may simply indicate that you need to wake up and go to the bathroom. Symbolically, the dream may indicate a desire to eliminate impurities from your life.

V

Vagrant Are you afraid of losing your home, stability, or livelihood? Perhaps you want to break away from social regimentation.

Valuables Uncovering valuables may symbolize the discovery of self-worth or inner resources.

Vampire To dream of a vampire may indicate that someone is draining energy from you or taking advantage of you. The message is to guard against people who take too much of your time or energy. To dream of battling or staking a vampire suggests a positive outcome versus someone with harmful intentions.

Vault A vault usually holds valuables. Your ability to open it determines the nature of the dream. If you hold the key, the vault may be a symbol of wealth and prosperity. If you are unable to open it, then the dream may signify that you are being frustrated in your effort to achieve wealth or a specific goal.

Veil A dream in which someone or something is veiled suggests that you're hiding something or something is being hidden from you.

Victim A dream of yourself as a victim may indicate that you're feeling helpless regarding a situation. If someone rescues you, the dream suggests that help is available.

Violin A violin played in a dream portends a romantic interlude, a time of love and harmony. It can also mean that you or someone else is "high strung."

Visitor Encountering a visitor in a dream indicates that a new condition is entering your life. If you welcome the visitor, the change may be for the better. If you turn away the visitor, you're unwilling to change or you don't accept what is being offered.

Volcano The eruption of a volcano or a smoking volcano may suggest that your strong emotions are rising to the surface and need to be expressed before you literally explode.

Vomit To vomit in a dream may be a dramatic exhibition of a need to rid something or someone from your life. To dream of vomiting a chicken suggests an illness in a relative will be a cause of disappointment. To see others vomiting symbolizes that someone's false pretenses will soon be made apparent.

W

Wallet A wallet carries personal effects, such as your identification. It is also where you carry financial resources. If you dream of losing your wallet, it may relate to a concern about your sense of self or about your finances. What happens in the dream and how you react can help you determine its meaning.

War A dream of war could relate to reliving your past in the military. Whether you've served in the military or not, a dream of war might symbolize internal turmoil or a need to make peace with yourself, or others. By examining other elements in the dream, you may determine the message behind the aggressive behavior.

Washing If you are washing something in a dream, you may be attempting to cleanse or purify the self. If a stain won't come out, the dream may relate to a concern about something from your past connected with feelings of guilt.

Water A dream of water can relate to the emotions or the unconscious. In the Freudian perspective, water relates to sexual matters, usually the female genitalia. (see Lake, Ocean, River, and Waves.)

Waterfall Water signifies the unconscious or the emotions, so to dream of waterfalls may represent a sudden or dramatic change in the dreamer's emotional state.

Waves Waves symbolize the power of the unconscious or emotions. Enormous breaking waves may represent powerful emotions, and gentle waves may suggest a tranquil state of mind.

Weapon Weapons may stand for the male genitals. The meaning of the dream is best determined by considering who is holding the weapon and how it is being used.

Wedding Weddings are a union between two people, and dreams of weddings may symbolize the joining or acceptance of your unconscious to an idea or emotion. To attend a wedding in a dream connotes an occasion that may bring about bitterness and delayed success. To dream of a wedding that is not approved by your parents suggests unrest among family members over a situation.

Weeds Dreaming of weeds suggests that something needs to be weeded out from your life. An overgrown garden might signify that something is being neglected in your life.

Well A well in a dream reveals that resources are available deep within you, although you may not be aware of it. To fall into a well symbolizes a loss of control regarding a matter at hand. A dry well indicates that you feel a part of your life is empty and needs to be nourished. To draw water from a well denotes the fulfillment of ardent desires.

Wet As in the saying "you're all wet," wetness represents uncertainty or a lack of knowledge. Maybe someone is giving you bad advice for a particular situation. For a young woman to dream that she is soaking wet symbolizes a disgraceful affair with someone who is already attached.

Whale A whale is an enormous mammal and to dream of one might indicate that you are dealing with a whale of a project. On the other hand, a whale dream may suggest you are overwhelmed. Whales can also relate to water and the relationship of the self to the unconscious and the emotions.

Whirlpool Water represents the emotions or the unconscious, so to dream of a whirlpool may indicate that your emotions are in a state of flux and can ensnarl you unless caution is exercised.

Whirlwind A dream of a whirlwind suggests that you are confronting a change in a matter at hand which threatens to overwhelm you. Pay attention to the other aspects of the dream. Are you facing this danger alone or with somebody? Are you in your house?

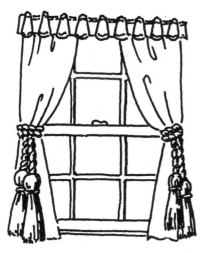

Window If a window appears in a dream, it may symbolize a view of your life from the inside out. Are there changes you would like to make? If the view is illuminated, then the outlook is bright. If you are on the outside looking in, you may feel that you have been excluded from something.

Wine Drinking wine in a dream might be a sign of celebration. It can also represent an elevated or altered state of mind. In a spiritual sense, wine can symbolize a transformation. For an alcoholic or someone who has been affected by one, wine or other alcoholic beverages can represent a negative influence.

Wings Wings are a means of transport and they may suggest that you will soar to wealth and honor, or that you are worried over someone who has gone on a long journey.

Witch How one sees a witch determines the meaning of a dream in which one appears. The Halloween image of a witch might be symbolic of a scary or evil scenario. For those involved in Wicca or attracted to New Age ideas, a witch might relate to the worship and respect of nature and the earth.

Wolf In Native American lore, the wolf is good medicine, a symbol of the pathfinder, a teacher with great wisdom and knowledge. Dreaming of a wolf can be auspicious. Alternately, the wolf can be a symbol of a lone male aggressively pursuing a young female as in the Little Red Riding Hood fable.

Woman The appearance of different types of women can symbolize different things in a dream. A dark-haired woman with blue eyes and a pug nose may represent a withdrawal from a matter at hand. A brown-eyed woman with a hook nose may suggest that you will be lured into a speculative venture. A woman who appears with auburn hair only adds to your anxiety over an issue. A blonde woman is symbolic of a favorable or pleasing outcome.

Writing Writing is usually difficult to read in a dream, so the message is usually symbolic. Writing could serve as a warning as in "the handwriting is on the wall." Writing could also suggest that your inner self is seeking to make contact with your conscious self. Ancient writings in a dream indicate that the dreamer is seeking knowledge from the distant past.

Y

Yard Dreaming of a yard may relate to your childhood, a time when you played in the yard. The dream may symbolize a

longing for a carefree time, for more personal space, or for something to fill the vacancy of the yard.

Yellow In the positive sense, yellow is the symbol of brightness, energy, and intellect. The color can also be linked to cowardice behavior.

Youth A dream of a youth might signify that you are being energized by those younger than you. Seeing yourself as younger in a dream may point to youthful self-empowerment.

Z

Zero A symbol of many interpretations, zero can mean emptiness, a lack of something in your life. It also forms a circle and can stand for wholeness and completion, or even the mysteries of the unknown. In Freudian terms, the shape is reminiscent of a vagina and suggests a desire for sexual relations.

Zoo A dream of a zoo might relate to a feeling of being in a cage. It could also symbolize chaos as in "The place is like a zoo." Alternately, it could recall a time of recreation, relaxation, and pleasure.

My Personal Glossary
Use this section to start your own glossary.

My Personal Glossary

APPENDIX A

Dream Groups

Here are a list of organizations and publications involved in dream-related activities.

Alfred Adler Institute
1780 Broadway
New York, NY 10019

The Alfred Adler Institute provides training in psychotherapy and counseling along the theory of individual psychology as formulated by Austrian psychiatrist Alfred Adler.

American Sleep Disorders Association
(ASDA)
1610 14th St. NW, Suite 300
Rochester, MN 55901

If you suffer from insomnia, night terrors, or any other sleep-related disorder, you might gain help from the ASDA. Referrals to sleep disorder centers in your area can be provided. These centers offer diagnostic and treatment services.

American Society for Psychical Research
5 W. 73rd St.
New York, NY 10023

The American Society for Psychical Research conducts research activities into the paranormal, including the telepathic influences on dreams.

Association for Research and
Enlightenment (A.R.E.)
PO Box 595
Virginia Beach, VA 23451

A.R.E., also known as the Edgar Cayce Foundation, offers an extensive research library based on the recorded readings of famed psychic Edgar Cayce. A.R.E. offers year-round seminars on a wide range of topics related to parapsychology, including dreams.

Association for the Study of Dreams (ASD)
PO Box 1600
Vienna, VA 22183

ASD provides an international forum for promoting research and dispensing information about the psychological and therapeutic aspects of dreams and their interpretation. The association offers a newsletter and sponsors conferences.

Atlantic University
67th St. and Atlantic Avenue
PO Box 595
Virginia Beach, VA 23451-0595

Atlantic University, an outgrowth of A.R.E., offers an accredited M.A. degree in transpersonal psychology as well as a wide range of at-home study courses or on-site courses in Virginia Beach.

Cleargreen, Inc.
11901 Santa Monica Blvd.
Suite 599
Los Angeles, CA 90025

Cleargreen was founded by Carlos Castaneda and his colleagues in sorcery to promote the teachings of don Juan Matus, a Yaqui Indian and sorcerer who taught dreaming techniques to Castaneda. The organization promotes seminars in which "magical passes," called Tensegrity, are taught. It publishes a newsletter, The Warriors' Way—a *Journal of Applied Hermeneutics*—several times a year.

Common Boundary
4304 East-West Highway
Bethesda, MD 20814

Common Boundary is an educational organization founded to foster support and communication for those in mental health, helping, and healing professions, and anyone interested in the interrelationships between psychology, spirituality, and creativity.

Community Dreamsharing Network
PO Box 8032
Hicksville, NY 11802

The Community Dreamsharing Network is an organization for individuals interested in discussing and understanding their dreams. It arranges local dreamsharing groups and encourages networking. It publishes *The Dream Switchboard*.

Dream Network
1137 Powerhouse Ln. Suite 22
Moab, UT 84532

Dream Network is a quarterly journal devoted to exploring the relationship between dreams and myths. Its stated purpose is to "demystify dream work and to integrate dream-sharing into our lives for the enhancement of our culture." The *Network* also provides information on ongoing dream groups.

C.G. Jung Foundation for Analytical Psychology
28.E. 39th St.
New York, NY 10016

The Jung Foundation offers training and information on analytical psychology based on Jungian concepts. Archival material includes studies on archetypal symbolism.

National Sleep Foundation
122 S. Robertson Blvd. 3rd FL.
Los Angeles, CA 90048

The National Sleep Foundation promotes education on sleep disorders, develops community resources, sponsors educational and research programs, and encourages local support groups.

Omega Institute
260 Lake Drive
Rhinebeck, NY 12572-3212

The Omega Institute offers seminars taught by the leaders in psychology, metaphysics, shamanism, the arts, and related fields. Write for a catalog.

The Pacific Northwest Center for Dream
    Studies
219 First Avenue S, Suite 405
Seattle, WA 98104

The Pacific Northwest Center offers dream work classes and psychotherapy using Jungian, Gestalt, and Delaney methods as well as ceremonial art forms.

The Saybrook Institute
1772 Vallejo Street
San Francisco, CA 94123

Founded and directed by Dr. Stanley Krippner, a renowned dream researcher and author, Saybrook is an accredited graduate school that offers students many opportunities to study dreams. Write for more information.

Seth Network International
P.O. Box 1620
Eugene, OR 97440

The Seth Network publishes *Reality Change* magazine, as well as books related to ideas put forth by Seth, the "energy personality essence" channeled by author Jane Roberts. The magazine and the organization explore the nature of consciousness and reality.

Sleep Research Society (SRS)
c/o Wallace Mendelson
Cleveland Clinic S-51
Dept. of Neurology
9500 Euclid Ave.
Cleveland, OH 44195

SRS conducts research into the study of sleep. It promotes and disseminates information on the physiological and psychological aspects of sleep. It publishes the bimonthly journal *Sleep*.

APPENDIX B

Books about Dreaming

Castaneda, C., *The Art of Dreaming*. New York, HarperCollins, 1993.

Delaney, G., *Breakthrough Dreaming: How to Tap the Power of Your 24-Hour Mind*. New York, Bantam, 1991.

Faraday, A., *Dream Power*. New York, Afar Publishers, 1972.

Faraday, A., *The Dream Game*. New York, Harper & Row, 1974.

Garfield, P., *Creative Dreaming*. New York, Ballantine, 1974.

Godwin, M., *The Lucid Dreamer*. New York, Simon & Schuster, 1994.

Harner, M., *The Way of the Shaman*. New York, Harper & Row, 1980.

Jung, C., *Man and His Symbols*. New York, Dell, 1964.

Jung, C., *Memories, Dreams, Reflections*. New York, Vintage, 1961.

LaBerge, S., *Lucid Dreaming*. New York, Ballantine, 1986.

LaBerge, S. and Rheingold, H., *Exploring the World of Lucid Dreaming*. New York, Random House, 1990.

Lewis, J., *The Dream Encyclopedia*. Detroit, Visible Ink Books, 1995.

Maxmen, J., *A Good Night's Sleep*. New York, Warner, 1981.

McGuire, W. and Hull, R. (Eds.), *C.G. Jung Speaking*. Princeton, N.J., Princeton University Press, 1977.

Michaels, S., *The Bedside Guide to Dreams*. New York, Fawcett Crest, 1995.

Morris, J., *The Dream Workbook*. New York, Fawcett Crest, 1985.

Perkins, J., *PsychoNavigation*. Rochester, Vt., Destiny Books, 1990.

Perkins, J., *The World as You Dream It: Shamanic Teachings from the Amazon and Andes*. Rochester, Vt., Destiny Books, 1994.

Roberts, J., *Seth Speaks*. New York, Prentice-Hall, 1972.

Roberts, J., *The Nature of Personal Reality: A Seth Book*. New York, Prentice-Hall, 1974.

Roberts, J., *Seth: Dreams and Projection of Consciousness*. New York, Prentice-Hall, 1987.

Sanford, J., *Dreams and Healing: A Succinct and Lively Interpretation of Dreams*. New York, Paulist Press, 1978.

Ullman, M. and Krippner, S. and Vaughan, A., *Dream Telepathy*. Toronto, Macmillan, 1973.

Ullman, M., Zimmerman, N., *Working with Dreams*. New York, Dell, 1979.

Villoldo, A., *Dance of the Four Winds*. New York, Harper & Row, 1990.

Villoldo, A., *Island of the Sun: Mastering the Inca Medicine Wheel*. San Francisco, HarperSanFrancisco, 1992.

Williams, S., *Jungian-Senoi Dreamwork Manual*. Berkeley, Journal Press, 1980.

INDEX